FOLLOWING GOD'S DIRECTION

JESUS CALLING BIBLE STUDY SERIES

Volume 1: Experiencing God's Presence

Volume 2: Trusting in Christ

Volume 3: Receiving Christ's Hope

Volume 4: Living a Life of Worship

Volume 5: Giving Thanks to God

Volume 6: Living with God's Courage

Volume 7: Dwelling in God's Peace

Volume 8: Putting Jesus First

JESUS ALWAYS BIBLE STUDY SERIES

Volume 1: Embracing Jesus' Love

Volume 2: Following God's Direction

Volume 3: Leading a Joy-Filled Life

Volume 4: Walking in God's Grace

JESUS ALWAYS BIBLE STUDY SERIES

FOLLOWING GOD'S DIRECTION

EIGHT SESSIONS

Sarah Young

with Karen Lee-Thorp

THOMAS NELSON
Since 1798

Published in Nashville, Tennessee, by Thomas Nelson. Thomas Nelson is a registered trademark of HarperCollins Christian Publishing, Inc.

All Scripture quotations, unless otherwise noted, are taken from The Holy Bible, New International Version®, NIV®. Copyright © 1973, 1978, 1984, 2011 by Biblica, Inc.® Used by permission. All rights reserved worldwide.

Scripture quotations marked ESV are taken from the ESV® (The Holy Bible, English Standard Version®). Copyright © 2001 by Crossway, a publishing ministry of Good News Publishers. Used by permission. All rights reserved.

Scripture quotations marked NKJV are taken from the New King James Version®. © 1982 by Thomas Nelson. Used by permission. All rights reserved.

ISBN 978-0-310-09135-6

First Printing January 2018 / Printed in the United States of America

CONTENTS

Introduction   vii

SESSION 1 FOLLOWING GOD BY TREASURING HIS WISDOM   1
   Proverbs 2:1–15, 20–22

SESSION 2 FOLLOWING GOD BY TRUSTING IN HIM   13
   Proverbs 3:1–18

SESSION 3 FOLLOWING GOD BY HONORING HIM   25
   Proverbs 9:1–12

SESSION 4 FOLLOWING GOD BY PRAYING FOR GUIDANCE   37
   James 1:5–8, 22–25

SESSION 5 FOLLOWING BY SHUNNING WORLDLY WISDOM   49
   James 3:13–18; 4:13–17

SESSION 6 FOLLOWING GOD BY LOVING HIS WORD   61
   Psalm 119:97–105

SESSION 7 FOLLOWING GOD BY LISTENING
TO THE SPIRIT OF TRUTH   73
   John 14:26; 16:12–15

SESSION 8 FOLLOWING GOD BY OBEYING
THE HOLY SPIRIT'S PROMPTINGS   85
   Acts 16:6–15

Leader's Notes   97

INTRODUCTION

Sometimes our busy and difficult lives give us the impression that God is silent. We cry out to Him, but our feelings tell us He isn't answering our prayers. In this, our feelings are incorrect. God hears the prayers of His children and speaks directly into the situations in which we find ourselves. The trouble is that our lives are often too hectic, our minds too distracted, for us to take in what He offers.

This *Jesus Always* Bible study is designed to help individuals and groups meditate on the words of Scripture and hear them not just as words said to people long ago but as words said to us today in the here and now. The goal is to help the heart open up and respond to what the mind reads—to encounter the living God as He speaks through the Scriptures. The writer to the Hebrews tells us:

In the past God spoke to our ancestors through the prophets at many times and in various ways, but in these last days he has spoken to us by his Son, whom he appointed heir of all things, and through whom also he made the universe. The Son is the radiance of God's glory and the exact representation of his being, sustaining all things by his powerful word.

—HEBREWS 1:1–3

God has spoken to us through His Son, Jesus Christ. The New Testament gives us the chance to walk with Jesus, see what He does, and hear Him speak into the sometimes-confusing situations in which we find ourselves. The Old Testament tells the story of how God prepared a people to be the family of Jesus, and in the experiences of those men and women, we find our own lives mirrored.

THE GOAL OF THIS SERIES

The *Jesus Always Bible Study Series* offers you a chance to lay down your cares, enter God's Presence, and hear Him speak through His Word. You will get to spend some time silently studying a passage of Scripture, and then, if you're meeting with a group, openly sharing your insights and hearing what others discovered. You'll also get to discuss excerpts from the *Jesus Always* devotional that relate to the themes of the Bible passages. In this way, you will learn how to better make space in your life for the Spirit of God to speak to you through the Word of God and the people of God.

THE FLOW OF EACH SESSION

Each session of this study guide contains the following elements:

- CONSIDER IT. The two questions in this opening section serve as an icebreaker to help you start thinking about the theme of the session, connecting it to your own past or present experience, and allowing you to get to know the others in your group more deeply. If you've had a busy day and your mind is full of distractions, these questions can help you better focus.

- EXPERIENCE IT. Here you will find two readings from *Jesus Always* along with some questions for reflection. This is your chance to talk with others about the biblical principles found within the *Jesus Always* devotions. Can you relate to what each reading describes? What insights from God's Word does it illuminate? What does it motivate you to do? This section will assist you in applying these biblical principles to your everyday habits.

- STUDY IT. Next you'll explore a Scripture passage connected to the session topic and the readings from *Jesus Always*. You will not only analyze these Bible passages but also pray through them in ways designed to engage your heart and your head. You'll first talk with your group about what the verse or verses mean and then spend several minutes in silence, letting God speak into your life through His Word.

- LIVE IT. Finally, you will find five days' worth of suggested Scripture passages that you can pray through on your own during the week. Suggested questions for additional study and reflection are provided.

FOR LEADERS

If you are leading a group through this study guide, please see the Leader's Notes at the end of the guide. You'll find background on the design of the study as well as suggested answers for some of the study questions.

FOLLOWING GOD BY TREASURING HIS WISDOM

CONSIDER IT

Each day we're deluged by *data*—the jumble of facts, pseudo-facts, thoughts, images, sounds, and opinions that floods our awareness every waking moment if we don't deliberately shut it out. With effort, we *can* organize and manage some portion of that data in a way that makes sense for us and helps us process our surroundings.

Most of us feel pretty good if we can contain some of the overflow at any given moment. But the biblical writers weren't impressed by mere information. They push us to think long and hard about what is truly important and then reflect only on the information that's valuable so we can honestly say we have *knowledge* about things that really matter. Beyond knowledge, the biblical writers urge us to pursue a heart-level understanding of how to live well in the world—and then put that understanding into practice. The word they use for applying this understanding to attain a life well lived is *wisdom*.

Wisdom doesn't always come quickly or effortlessly. It can't be downloaded. But if we want to learn to discern God's direction, the place to start is by setting our sights on wisdom. In this session, we'll begin to consider what wisdom is and how we can attain it.

1. *What are some of the sources of information that pour into your life each day?*

Friends, family, Social Media, News, Media

2. *How does all this information affect you? How does it influence your ability to discern what God might be saying to you?*

What's deemed societally as normal is diff. than God's standards. It's easy to justify living as the world does.

EXPERIENCE IT

I am your Treasure! Sometimes you feel frazzled—pulled this way and that by people and circumstances around you. Your yearning for meaning and deep connection drives you into more and more activity. Even when your body is still, your mind tends to race—anticipating future problems and searching for solutions. You need to remember that *all the treasures of wisdom and knowledge are hidden in Me*. Remind yourself of this glorious truth frequently, whispering: "Jesus, You are my Treasure. In You I am complete."

When you prize Me above all else, making Me your *First Love*, you are protected from feeling fragmented. Whenever you find your thoughts straying, you can train your mind to return to the One who completes you. This gives focus to your life and helps you stay close to Me. Living near Me, enjoying My Presence, involves seeking to *obey My commands*. I am telling you this *so that My Joy may be in you and that your Joy may be complete*.

—FROM *JESUS ALWAYS*, JANUARY 9

3. *In Genesis 15:1, God told Abraham, "I am your . . . exceedingly great reward" (NKJV). What does it mean to uphold God as your great reward? In what way is He your treasure?*

That even if I lost everything and never recieved anything else that I am still blessed because I always have God. He is my peace, protector, provider.

4. *According to the Bible, why is turning to Jesus the best way to deal with problems versus letting your mind race about potential solutions?*

Our flesh always wants to sin. The spirit wants to do right, so connecting with Jesus will guide us to what we should do

I guide you in the way of wisdom and lead you along straight paths. Wisdom can be defined as "the ability to make good decisions based on knowledge and experience." So it's important to learn what is true and apply that knowledge to your life—especially your decisions. Since *I am the Way, the Truth, and the Life,* I'm the best Guide imaginable. I am also *the Word* who *was with God and is God.* The way of wisdom found in the written Word guides you very effectively. So study My Word and stay near Me as you journey through this world.

Look for and follow the *straight paths* I have for you. I don't promise that these paths will always be easy. But if you walk close to Me, your journey will be much less circuitous. When you look ahead, you perceive confusing bends and turns. Yet when you look back at the ground you've already covered, you can see that I have been with you each step of the way—shielding you from dangers, removing obstacles, straightening out your path.

—FROM *JESUS ALWAYS,* JUNE 19

5. *As you look back at your life, what good and not-so-good decisions do you see? Would you say you've been developing wisdom over time? Explain.*

Definitely developing wisdom over time. I've made the same repeated mistakes which is upsetting and disappointing but I did notice that I end them quicker now.

6. *How do you go about learning what is true?*

By speaking the positive opposite of whatever lie or negative thought is being heard.

STUDY IT

Read aloud the following verses from Proverbs 2:1–15, 20–22. As you do, note that the book of Proverbs is framed as wise counsel from a father to a son. Before the father gives advice about things such as money, friends, and success, he begins by motivating his son to listen closely to what he has to say. He wants to encourage young readers everywhere to value wisdom. Also, he writes in Hebrew poetry, in which the two halves of each verse echo one another. The second half builds on the idea from the first half as it repeats the core idea of the verse.

¹ My son, if you accept my words
　　and store up my commands within you,
² turning your ear to wisdom
　　and applying your heart to understanding—
³ indeed, if you call out for insight
　　and cry aloud for understanding,
⁴ and if you look for it as for silver
　　and search for it as for hidden treasure,
⁵ then you will understand the fear of the LORD
　　and find the knowledge of God.
⁶ For the LORD gives wisdom;
　　from his mouth come knowledge and understanding.
⁷ He holds success in store for the upright,
　　he is a shield to those whose walk is blameless,
⁸ for he guards the course of the just
　　and protects the way of his faithful ones.
⁹ Then you will understand what is right and just
　　and fair—every good path.
¹⁰ For wisdom will enter your heart,
　　and knowledge will be pleasant to your soul.
¹¹ Discretion will protect you,
　　and understanding will guard you.

¹² Wisdom will <u>save you</u> from the ways of <u>wicked men</u>,

>from <u>men</u> whose words are perverse,

¹³ who have left the straight paths

>to walk in dark ways,

¹⁴ who delight in doing wrong

>and rejoice in the perverseness of evil,

¹⁵ whose paths are crooked

>and who are devious in their ways. . . .

²⁰ Thus you will <u>walk in</u> the ways of the good

>and <u>keep to the paths of the righteous.</u>

²¹ For the upright will live in the land,

>and the blameless will remain in it;

²² but the wicked will be cut off from the land,

>and the unfaithful will be torn from it.

7. *Underline the verbs in each line of verses 1–5. How does the writer want his reader to treat wisdom? Why do you think he wants the reader to do this?*

Accept, Store Up, Apply, Call out, Cry aloud, look for, Search. These are different stages we might be in when asking. Asking but not doing, not having scripture ready in mind, not using it, reading desperately, not seeing it, Ammo for any scenario.

8. *According to verses 6–8, to whom does the Lord give wisdom? What does it mean to be "blameless"?*

Upright, blameless, faithful. He means blameless because as true believers we have faith is Jesus sacrifice and therefore become blameless in the eyes of God.

9. *What will wisdom do for those who heed it, according to verses 11–15 and 20–22? How does wisdom accomplish this?*

Protect & Gaurd/Save you from the Wicked. Keeps you on good & righteous paths.

10. *How can a person look for wisdom "as for silver" and search for it "as for hidden treasure" (verse 4)?*

By meditating on and reading the word of God and asking God for it through Prayer.

11. *How does the Bible provide instructions from God about what we are to do and not do in any given situation?*

God speaks clearly and unchangingly on how we should react ~~to~~ or behave while in this world.

12. *Take two minutes of silence to reread the passage, looking for a sentence, phrase, or even one word that stands out as something Jesus may want you to focus on in your life. If you're meeting with a group, the leader will keep track of time. At the end of two minutes, you may share with the group the word or phrase that came to you in the silence.*

The part about being able to protect/guard/save myself from Sly talking wicked men is precisely what I needed right now.
-Perverse men?   -Like in land?   Jesus Jesus
                        Be cut off?   Jesus Jesus
                                      Jesus Jesus

13. *Read the passage aloud again. Take another two minutes of silence, prayerfully considering what response God might want you to make to what you have read in His Word. If you're meeting with a group, the leader will again keep track of time. At the end of two minutes, you may share with the group what came to you in the silence if you wish.*

This is not going to be easy but it will be worth it and EVERYTHING is possible with GOD.

14. *If you're meeting with a group, how can the members pray for you? If you're using this study on your own, what would you like to say to God right now?*

I know the focus of this year is STRONGER but I feel weaker than ever. God I need divine intervention, I cannot make these changes on my own, I welcome and accept it. And will act.

LIVE IT

At the end of each session, you'll find suggested Scripture readings for spending time alone with God during five days of the coming week. This week's readings are focused on obtaining biblical wisdom. Read each passage slowly, pausing to think about what is being said. Rather than approaching this as an assignment to complete, think of it as an opportunity to meet with the One who loves you most. Use any of the questions that are helpful.

Day 1

Read Colossians 2:1–4. In the New Testament, a "mystery" (verse 2) is something God has kept as a secret for a long time but has now revealed (or will reveal someday). What do you think Paul means when he says that all the treasures of wisdom and knowledge are hidden in Christ (verse 3)?

The cheat code to life, is through knowing Christ.

Why does Paul want the Colossians to understand the mystery of Christ (see verse 4)?

So that they will remain encouraged and not be decieved by fancy talk.

What are some "riches" of understanding that you want God to reveal to you today?

How to sacrifice my fleshly desires, to have discipline, and endurance So be stronger and pure.

Thank God today for revealing the "mystery" of Christ to His children.

Day 2

Read Colossians 1:9–12. How do God's children come to understand His will (see verse 9)?

Through prayer and the wisdom & understanding his Spirit gives. *(Pray for God's will not what I want)*

Why does God give Christians the knowledge of His will (see verse 10)? Is His goal to make life as easy as possible for His children? Why or why not?

To live a life that honors the LORD and come to know him better. Not easy. to send endure. You will be happy but

Paul speaks in verse 11 about endurance and patience. How do you think wisdom strengthens a believer's endurance and patience?

When you apply the knowledge that you have in God's ways you become unbothered and find peace in God's abilities. Remember what happened atside of God

Pray to receive the wisdom and understanding the Holy Spirit provides. Ask Him to help you lead a life worthy of Christ.

Day 3

Read Colossians 1:25–29. Paul speaks not just of the mystery of Christ but also of the mystery of Christ in believers. If you're a devoted follower of Jesus, in what way is "Christ in you" a secret that has now been revealed?

Life's purpose for us as believers. To share God's love and Jesus' sacrifice.

What does it mean to admonish someone with wisdom (verse 28)?

Alert and equip them. So all Christ's followers will grow & become mature.

When have you been admonished with wisdom? How did that affect you?

It feels peaceful and heavy at the same time. Like it's sunk in and you may ignore it but you'll never not know/understand that piece of wisdom again.

Listen today for the Lord's guiding voice of wisdom. Pay attention to Him in your circumstances.

Day 4

Read Ephesians 1:17–20. Why does Paul refer to the Holy Spirit as "the Spirit of wisdom and revelation" (verse 17)? What does that tell you about the Spirit?

Jesus tells us after res. that the spirit is here on earth to do just those things. When were w/o God our spirit is dead w/ God through the Spirit we are awakened to our true identity

The main point of growing in wisdom is to know God better (verse 17). How does knowing God lead to better decisions?

Think about this word picture: "that the eyes of your heart may be enlightened" (verse 18). What do you think "the eyes of your heart" means? Why are the eyes of the heart so important?

Spirituality
Door way to faith of what cannot be seen.

Look for a time today to use the "eyes of your heart." In that situation, ask God to enlighten you and guide you through it.

Day 5

Read Ecclesiastes 7:11–12. How is wisdom like an inheritance of money?

Inheritance - it was stored up and earned by someone before us (Jesus) Not earned
Shelter - security money is security

How is wisdom better than inheriting money?

Choices tru make money or do anythi to be successful.
than

Which do you tend to value more: wisdom or money? What is the evidence?

Ask God to help you treat wisdom as more valuable than money. Watch for a time to put that into practice during your day.

FOLLOWING GOD BY TRUSTING IN HIM

CONSIDER IT

Think back to the first time you used the maps app on your phone to guide you to an unfamiliar location. Perhaps you were a bit nervous about blindly following that friendly, computer-generated voice. Over time, though, you got used to it. You found the little voice on the phone was generally reliable. And it was not only easier than copying down directions before you went anywhere but safer than reading a map as you drove.

You grew to trust it. Yet there came a day when you typed in "2016 Alder Road"—unaware that there was a "2016 *North* Alder Road" and a "2016 *South* Alder Road." When you ended up miles from your intended destination, you resolved to never trust the little voice again. But what choice did you have? Were you really going to go back to mapping out directions ahead of time, every time?

In this session, we'll see that trusting guidance from God requires even greater faith than relying on a phone app. Sometimes the directions seem confusing, but what is the alternative? Trusting our own instincts will only leave us more lost in our life's journey.

1. *Think about your experiences with following the GPS on your phone. What was one good or bad experience you had with it?*

Getting lost while working for Toyota

2. *How is trusting God for guidance like trusting a map app on your phone? How is it different?*

Don't know the end destination, God takes you different routes to diff. places in our lives

EXPERIENCE IT

Relax, My child. I'm in control. Let these words wash over you repeatedly, like soothing waves on a beautiful beach, assuring you of My endless Love. You waste a lot of time and energy trying to figure out things before their time has come. Meanwhile, I am working to prepare the way before you. So be on the lookout for some wonderful surprises—circumstances that only *I* could have orchestrated.

Remember that you are My beloved. I am on your side, and I want what is best for you. Someone who is loved by a generous, powerful person can expect to receive an abundance of blessings. *You* are loved by the King of the universe, and I have good plans for you. As you look ahead into the unknown future, relax in the knowledge of who you are—*the one I love.* Cling to My hand, and go forward with confidence. While you and I walk together along *the path of Life,* your trust in Me will fill your heart with Joy and your mind with Peace.

—FROM *JESUS ALWAYS,* JANUARY 26

3. *How does it help you to reflect on the fact that God is in control of the lives of His children?*

Unbothered

4. *What does clinging to Jesus' hand look like for you in your present circumstances?*

Reading, Praising

There is a time for everything, and a season for every activity under heaven. When you seek My Face and My will—searching for guidance—I may show you the next step on your journey without revealing the appointed time for you to take that step. Instead of going full speed ahead as soon as you know what is next, you must wait until I show you *when* I want you to go forward.

There is a season for everything. This means that even the most fulfilling times in life must eventually give way to something new. Whereas some of My followers "champ at the bit" to forge ahead into new territory, others hold back even when I am clearly directing them to go forward. Moving from a comfortable season of life into a new situation can feel scary—especially to those who dislike change. However, I want you to trust Me enough to cling to Me and follow wherever I lead, *whenever* I choose. *Your times are in My hands.*

—From *Jesus Always*, January 11

5. *When have you had to wait for God's timing in some endeavor? How did you know when it was time to take action?*

_____

_____

_____

_____

6. *Do you tend to look forward to change, or to resist it? How can knowing this about yourself help you respond to God's timing?*

_____

_____

_____

_____

Study It

Read aloud the following passage from Proverbs 3:1–18. Once again we are listening to a father give counsel to his son. But this time, instead of just exhorting his son to cry aloud for wisdom, the father gives specific, wise principles that can guide his son's choices. For example, in verse 3, the father points out that when his son is not sure what to do, the right course is to choose love and faithfulness. Doing the loving thing is always a good rule of thumb to follow!

¹ My son, do not forget my teaching,
> but keep my commands in your heart,
² for they will prolong your life many years
> and bring you peace and prosperity.

³ Let love and faithfulness never leave you;
> bind them around your neck,
> write them on the tablet of your heart.
⁴ Then you will win favor and a good name
> in the sight of God and man.
⁵ Trust in the LORD with all your heart
> and lean not on your own understanding;
⁶ in all your ways submit to him,
> and he will make your paths straight.
⁷ Do not be wise in your own eyes;
> fear the LORD and shun evil.
⁸ This will bring health to your body
> and nourishment to your bones.
⁹ Honor the LORD with your wealth,
> with the firstfruits of all your crops;
¹⁰ then your barns will be filled to overflowing,
> and your vats will brim over with new wine.
¹¹ My son, do not despise the LORD's discipline,
> and do not resent his rebuke,

[handwritten note: You'll be okay!]

¹² because the LORD disciplines those he loves,

    as a father the son he delights in.

¹³ Blessed are those who find wisdom,

    those who gain understanding,

¹⁴ for she is more profitable than silver

    and yields better returns than gold.

¹⁵ She is more precious than rubies;

    nothing you desire can compare with her.

¹⁶ Long life is in her right hand;

    in her left hand are riches and honor.

¹⁷ Her ways are pleasant ways,

    and all her paths are peace.

¹⁸ She is a tree of life to those who take hold of her;

    those who hold her fast will be blessed.

7. *What is faithfulness (verse 3)? Why is this such an important quality to cultivate?*

Win favor to God/Man, God is the giver
Belief in things unseen.
Stedfast Consistent

8. *Why is trusting in the Lord with all your heart so much smarter than leaning on your own understanding (verses 5–6)?*

Our understanding is limited
God is not
It'll bring health to your body &
nurishment to bones

9. *What does it mean to be wise in your own eyes (verse 7)? What's wrong with this attitude?*

Fleshly desires vs Spirit desires

10. *Verse 9 says to "Honor the LORD with your wealth." How is this an example of trusting the Lord?*

Tithing

11. *How does discipline (verses 11–12) contribute to growth in wisdom?*

12. *Take two minutes of silence to reread the passage, looking for a sentence, phrase, or even one word that stands out as something Jesus may want you to focus on in your life. If you're meeting with a group, the leader will keep track of time. At the end of two minutes, you may share with the group the word or phrase that came to you in the silence.*

13. *Read the passage aloud again. Take another two minutes of silence, prayerfully considering what response God might want you to make to what you have read in His Word. If you're meeting with a group, the leader will again keep track of time. At the end of two minutes, you may share with the group what came to you in the silence if you wish.*

_____

_____

_____

_____

14. *If you're meeting with a group, how can the members pray for you? If you're using this study on your own, what would you like to say to God right now?*

_____

_____

_____

_____

LIVE IT

This week's readings are focused on the connection between trusting in God and receiving His wisdom. Read each passage slowly, pausing to think about what is being said. Rather than approaching this as an assignment to complete, think of it as an opportunity to meet with the One who loves you most. Use any of the questions that are helpful.

Day 1

Read Proverbs 4:5–9. Why do you suppose the writer of Proverbs keeps repeating his instruction to get wisdom no matter what? Why does this have to be repeated?

It seems like wisdom is hard to truly recieve but it is greatly important. Verses 7

What are the benefits of wisdom, according to this passage?

Exalt you, grace, glory Protection.

Do you trust this is the best advice you could live by? What's the evidence?

Keep asking God for wisdom as you go through your day.

Day 2

Read Proverbs 28:25–26. In verse 25, notice the contrast between greed and trust. How are these actually opposites? What does this tell you about greed?

Greed is trying to provide for yourself by any means. Trust is giving all your cares to God by all means! Greed is a lonely feeling because your working in your own strength.

21

Is greed a problem in your life? What's the evidence?

Srumy.

Consider verse 26. What does the writer mean when he states that those who walk in wisdom are "kept safe"?

Out of Gods provision

Pay attention to your attitude toward money and possessions. Notice if you are tempted to trust what you own more than the One who owns you.

Day 3

Read Proverbs 21:22. What claim does this proverb make about wisdom?

The power of wisdom

How can wisdom be greater than a fortified city? What gives wisdom that power?

How diligent are you in seeking wisdom? Why do you think that's the case?

If you feel weak, pursue wisdom today. Ask the Lord how to do that.

Day 4

Proverbs 23:4 says, "Do not trust your own cleverness." What are some of the ways in the past that you've fallen victim to trusting in your own cleverness?

What was the result of your actions? What did you learn from the experience?

In what area of your life do you currently need to stop trusting in your own cleverness?

MEN!!

Look for a specific opportunity to trust the Lord's wisdom today, and ask Him to make that opportunity clear.

Day 5

Read Proverbs 29:25. What do you think the "fear of man" means?

Earthly Things

How does the "fear of man" get expressed in a person's thoughts and actions?

Making made fear cause the fr go against Gods Plans

In what ways is the fear of man a snare?

If the fear of man tempts you today, seek God's help in overcoming it.

FOLLOWING GOD BY HONORING HIM

CONSIDER IT

Terrorists . . . viruses . . . tornadoes . . . crime—the world is filled with bad things that can cause us to fear. Even when we read God's instructions to "be strong and courageous" (Joshua 1:9), "not worry about tomorrow" (Matthew 6:34), and "do not be afraid" (John 14:27), it can be difficult to put them into practice and not give into fear. But the Bible is clear on what we are to fear—and it is not anything in this world.

In Luke 12:4–5, Jesus made this startling statement to His followers: "I tell you, my friends, do not be afraid of those who kill the body and after that can do no more. But I will show you whom you should fear: Fear him who, after your body has been killed, has authority to throw you into hell. Yes, I tell you, fear him." Then, in the next breath, He adds, "Are not five sparrows sold for two pennies? Yet not one of them is forgotten by God. Indeed, the very hairs of your head are all numbered. Don't be afraid" (Luke 12:6–7).

Jesus was saying that if we fear God—if we show respect and honor to Him—we don't need to fear anything else. We are to fear God but at the same time not be afraid of anything in this world, because we are of value to Him. In this session, we'll explore what it means to have a healthy fear, awe, and respect for the One who loves us.

1. *What is something you appropriately fear or respect?*

---

2. *Is there anything you fear that you shouldn't fear? If so, what is it?*

EXPERIENCE IT

I delight in those who fear Me, who put their hope in My unfailing Love. "Fear of the Lord" is often misunderstood, but it is the foundation of spiritual wisdom and knowledge. It consists of reverential awe, adoration, and submission to My will. You submit to Me by exchanging *your* attitudes and goals for *Mine*. Since I am your Creator, aligning yourself with Me is the best way to live. When your lifestyle exhibits this biblical fear, I take delight in you. Seek to feel My pleasure shining on you at such times.

Living according to My will is not easy; there will be many ups and downs as you journey with Me. But no matter what is happening, you can find hope in My unfailing Love. In your world today, many people are feeling desperate. They've become disillusioned and cynical because they put their confidence in the wrong thing. But *My steadfast Love* will never let you down—it will never let you go! Cling to hope, beloved. It's a golden cord connecting you to Me.

—FROM *JESUS ALWAYS*, SEPTEMBER 17

3. *In Psalm 112:1, we read, "Blessed are those who fear the* LORD, *who find great delight in his commands." Why do you suppose God blesses those who fear Him?*

_____

_____

_____

4. *What is one of God's attitudes or goals that you have already taken on or are trying to take on?*

_____

_____

_____

Ask Me for wisdom, beloved. I know how much you need it! King Solomon requested *a discerning heart*, and he received wisdom in magnificent abundance. This precious gift is also essential for you, especially when you're making plans and decisions. So come to Me for what you need, and *trust Me* to provide it in full measure.

One aspect of wisdom is recognizing your need for My help in all that you do. When your mind is sluggish, it's easy to forget about Me and simply dive into your tasks and activities. But eventually you bump into an obstacle. Then you face an important choice: to push ahead full throttle or to stop and ask Me for insight, understanding, and guidance. The closer to Me you live, the more readily and frequently you will seek My help.

The fear of the Lord is the beginning of wisdom. Though I am your Friend, remember who I am in My *great Power and Glory*! Godly fear—reverential awe and worshipful admiration—provides the best foundation for wisdom.

—FROM *JESUS ALWAYS*, OCTOBER 6

5. *What is an area of your life where you currently need wisdom? Have you asked God for it?*

_____

_____

_____

6. *What are some of the reasons we often don't immediately go to God for insight?*

_____

_____

_____

STUDY IT

Read aloud the following passage from Proverbs 9:1–12. In these verses, the writer envisions wisdom as a woman inviting the "simple" to a feast. The simple are those individuals who haven't yet developed wisdom but have the potential to do so. They are spiritual adolescents, vulnerable to deception and temptation. They are different from "the mockers" described in verses 7–8, who have deliberately rejected wisdom. Lady Wisdom is primarily calling the simple and uninformed to come to her feast and learn the fear of the Lord.

1 Wisdom has built her house;
   she has set up its seven pillars.
2 She has prepared her meat and mixed her wine;
   she has also set her table.
3 She has sent out her servants, and she calls
   from the highest point of the city,
4 "Let all who are simple come to my house!"
   To those who have no sense she says,
5 "Come, eat my food
   and drink the wine I have mixed.
6 Leave your simple ways and you will live;
   walk in the way of insight."
7 Whoever corrects a mocker invites insults;
   whoever rebukes the wicked incurs abuse.
8 Do not rebuke mockers or they will hate you;
   rebuke the wise and they will love you.
9 Instruct the wise and they will be wiser still;
   teach the righteous and they will add to their learning.
10 The fear of the LORD is the beginning of wisdom,
   and knowledge of the Holy One is understanding.
11 For through wisdom your days will be many,
   and years will be added to your life.
12 If you are wise, your wisdom will reward you;
   if you are a mocker, you alone will suffer.

7. *Why isn't it okay to just remain one of the simple?*

8. *What do you learn about Wisdom by thinking of her as a lady offering a feast?*

9. *Why do you suppose the fear of the Lord is the beginning of wisdom (see verse 10)? Why not the love of the Lord?*

10. *Why are the wise grateful for rebuke and advice (see verses 8–9)?*

11. *Verse 10 pairs the fear of the Lord with knowledge of the Holy One. How are these two qualities connected? Why is it important for God's children to maintain a healthy fear of Him even though they recognize that their sins have been forgiven?*

---

12. *Take two minutes of silence to reread the passage, looking for a sentence, phrase, or even one word that stands out as something Jesus may want you to focus on in your life. If you're meeting with a group, the leader will keep track of time. At the end of two minutes, you may share with the group the word or phrase that came to you in the silence.*

---

13. *Read the passage aloud again. Take another two minutes of silence, prayerfully considering what response God might want you to make to what you have read in His Word. If you're meeting with a group, the leader will again keep track of time. At the end of two minutes, you may share with the group what came to you in the silence if you wish.*

---

14. *If you're meeting with a group, how can the members pray for you? If you're using this study on your own, what would you like to say to God right now?*

_____

_____

_____

LIVE IT

This week's readings are focused on the theme of "fearing" and honoring the Lord. Read each passage slowly, pausing to think about what is being said. Rather than approaching this as an assignment to complete, think of it as an opportunity to meet with the One who loves you most. Use any of the questions that are helpful.

Day 1

Read Exodus 14:26–31. The Israelites have been fleeing the Egyptian army. They have gone as far as the sea, and now they think they are trapped. But then the Lord parts the waters so they can walk across the sea bed. Why do you think this incident moved them to fear the Lord and not simply be grateful?

_____

_____

_____

How did the Israelites' fear of the Lord lead to them trusting in Him?

_____

_____

_____

What has the Lord done for you that has inspired—or should inspire—a
healthy fear of Him?

Look back through your life and around you in the world for signs of
God's power. Let these evoke awe and reverence for Him.

Day 2

Read 2 Chronicles 19:4–7. Why is it important that judges fear the Lord?

How would our world be different if judges everywhere feared the Lord?

How would the fear of the Lord be a good quality for other people in authority,
including parents and bosses?

Consider the areas of your life where you have authority and identify one way the fear of the Lord can improve the way you fulfill your role.

Day 3

Read Psalm 19:7–9. Why do you suppose the psalmist includes the fear of the Lord in this list that otherwise includes the law, statutes, precepts, commands, and decrees of the Lord? What does the fear of the Lord have to do with those?

_____

_____

_____

What does it mean to say the fear of the Lord is pure or clean? How does it endure forever?

_____

_____

_____

How have you grown in your fear of the Lord after thinking about it so much? Describe where it fits in your life.

_____

_____

_____

Ask the Holy Spirit today to properly strengthen your fear of the Lord.

Day 4

Read Psalm 25:12–15. How does the psalmist connect the fear of the Lord with the Lord's direction in the lives of His sons and daughters (see verse 12)?

What other benefits of the fear of the Lord does the psalmist mention?

Why does the Lord confide in those who fear Him and not in those who don't (see verse 14)?

Offer a prayer to God today that expresses your respect for Him and your desire that He be with you in the midst of situations that can cause you fear.

Day 5

Read Psalm 33:6–9. What does the fear of the Lord have to do with the Lord as Creator?

_____

_____

_____

What helps remind you that the Lord made everything around you?

_____

_____

_____

What can get in the way of remembering that God is the Artist who made the universe?

_____

_____

_____

Take some time to praise God as Creator of everything that exists. Let that feed your reverence for Him.

FOLLOWING GOD BY PRAYING FOR GUIDANCE

CONSIDER IT

In traditional medieval churches, the part of the church where the congregation stood or sat was called the nave, from the Latin word *navis*, meaning "ship." The ceiling of the nave was vaulted and looked much like an upside-down ship. The idea was that the Christian community was much like Noah's ark, carrying believers through deep and choppy waters to safety.

God wants to help His children navigate the often-churning waters in which they find themselves. He wants them to know they're not all alone in a one-person vessel on the sea. They're in a big ship, and they have God Himself as their pilot if they let Him do His job.

So, how do the people of God access His help? In this session, we'll see that the main thing to do is simply ask Him with faith. Asking Him from a state of panic or cynicism won't do. If you're a believer, you can go into prayer simply believing God is a good Father who longs to guide you through the storm.

1. *How would you describe the waters you're currently sailing? Explain your answer below.*
   - ☐ Calm and clear (great sailing)
   - ☐ Doldrums (stagnant)
   - ☐ Choppy (a little rough)
   - ☐ Stormy (danger on the horizon)
   - ☐ Hurricane conditions (emergency!)

2. *What is one question about your life that you wish you could ask God?*

EXPERIENCE IT

I am training you not only to endure your difficulties but to transform them into Glory. This is a supernatural feat, and it requires the help of My supernatural Spirit. When problems are weighing heavily on you, your natural tendency is to speed up your pace of living, frantically searching for answers. But what you need at such times is to *slow down* and seek My Face. Invite the Spirit to help you as you discuss your difficulties with Me. Then *lay your requests before Me and wait in expectation.*

Even though you wait expectantly, I may not answer your prayers quickly. I am always doing something important in your life—far beyond simply solving your problems. Your struggles are part of a much larger battle, and the way you handle them can contribute to outcomes with eternal significance. When you respond to your troubles by trusting Me and *praying with thanksgiving,* you glorify Me. Moreover, your practice of praying persistently will eventually make a vast difference in you—My loved one *crowned with Glory.*

—FROM *JESUS ALWAYS,* MARCH 21

3. *What do you typically do when problems weigh heavily on you?*

_____

_____

_____

4. *Why is a godly response so important in times of trouble?*

_____

_____

_____

Before you begin a task—large or small—take time to pray about it. By doing so, you acknowledge your need for Me and your trust that I will help you. This enables you to go about your work in dependence on Me. There are many benefits to this practice. I can guide your mind as you think things out and make decisions. Just knowing I am involved in what you're doing gives you confidence, reducing stress. It's wise to thank Me often for My help and to keep asking Me to *guide you along the best pathway*.

Though the Bible instructs you to *pray continually*, at times you ignore this teaching. When you're feeling rushed, you find it hard to slow down enough to seek My perspective on the work at hand. However, diving in and forging ahead on your own is actually counterproductive. When you request My involvement *before* you begin, I can point you in the right direction—saving precious time and energy. I delight in helping you with everything, even simple tasks, because you are *My beloved*.

—FROM *JESUS ALWAYS*, FEBRUARY 16

5. *What are some benefits of Christians taking time to pray about a task before launching into it?*

_____

_____

_____

_____

6. *In 1 Thessalonians 5:17, Paul instructs Christians to "pray continually." If this is so helpful for followers of Christ, why do we often fail to do it?*

_____

_____

_____

_____

Study It

Read aloud the following passage from James 1:5–8, 22–25. Like the books of Proverbs, Ecclesiastes, and Job, the book of James is generally about wisdom—about how to live rather than what to believe. James assumes everything the New Testament teaches about Jesus' birth, death, resurrection, and ascension to be true, and he's interested in helping readers live in light of those facts. One word James uses (which he may have coined) is *double-minded*, which means restlessly being pulled in opposing directions in our thoughts, feelings, and actions. James also speaks of the gospel as "the perfect law that gives freedom" in contrast to the Old Testament law, which burdened people.

> [5] If any of you lacks wisdom, you should ask God, who gives generously to all without finding fault, and it will be given to you. [6] But when you ask, you must believe and not doubt, because the one who doubts is like a wave of the sea, blown and tossed by the wind. [7] That person should not expect to receive anything from the Lord. [8] Such a person is double-minded and unstable in all they do. . . .
>
> [22] Do not merely listen to the word, and so deceive yourselves. Do what it says. [23] Anyone who listens to the word but does not do what it says is like someone who looks at his face in a mirror [24] and, after looking at himself, goes away and immediately forgets what he looks like. [25] But whoever looks intently into the perfect law that gives freedom, and continues in it—not forgetting what they have heard, but doing it—they will be blessed in what they do.

7. James says that when we ask for wisdom, Christians need to believe and not doubt. What do you do, however, when you have doubts as to whether God will really come through for you?

---

8. *Do you have any doubts about God that make it hard for you to pray? If so, what are they?*

9. *Why do you think God refrains from supplying wisdom to His children until they ask for it in faith?*

10. *According to verses 22–25, how should you interact with the Word of God, the Bible, if you sincerely want direction from God?*

11. *The gospel, being "the perfect law that gives freedom" (verse 25), isn't just something to believe but also something to do. What are some examples of things the Bible asks Christians to do?*

12. *Take two minutes of silence to reread the passage, looking for a sentence, phrase, or even one word that stands out as something Jesus may want you to focus on in your life. If you're meeting with a group, the leader will keep track of time. At the end of two minutes, you may share with the group the word or phrase that came to you in the silence.*

13. *Read the passage aloud again. Take another two minutes of silence, prayerfully considering what response God might want you to make to what you have read in His Word. If you're meeting with a group, the leader will again keep track of time. At the end of two minutes, you may share with the group what came to you in the silence if you wish.*

14. *If you're meeting with a group, how can the members pray for you? If you're using this study on your own, what would you like to say to God right now?*

LIVE IT

This week's readings are focused on the theme of seeking God's guidance in matters involving your speech, your pride, your friends and advisers, your patience and perseverance, and your temper. Read each passage slowly, pausing to think about what is being said. Rather than approaching this as an assignment to complete, think of it as an opportunity to meet with the One who loves you most. Use any of the questions that are helpful.

Day 1

Read Proverbs 10:31–32. Why do you think righteousness and wisdom are connected?

What is meant by "a perverse tongue [that] will be silenced" (verse 31)?

Both Proverbs and James say much about how to use your tongue. Why do you suppose that's of such great concern to those who write about wisdom?

Pay attention to what comes out of your mouth today, as well as what you say in your texts and social media. Examine whether any of it is unfitting.

Day 2

Read Proverbs 11:2. How would you define pride? What is wrong with it?

_____

_____

_____

How is pride different from a healthy self-respect?

_____

_____

_____

How is humility different from humiliation?

_____

_____

_____

Ask the Lord to reveal any ungodly pride you may have and to help you grow in humility.

Day 3

Read Proverbs 11:13–14. How does the writer describe a trustworthy person?

_____

_____

_____

Why is it wise to take advice from trustworthy people?

_____

_____

_____

Who do you trust to advise you? What makes them trustworthy?

_____

_____

_____

Seek advice today from someone you respect. Solicit their feedback about some area of your life in which you have questions.

Day 4

Read Proverbs 15:32–33. What does the writer say about those who disregard discipline? How is this surprising statement true?

_____

_____

_____

Why is humility such an important component in acting wisely (see verse 33)?

_____

_____

_____

How does humility open the way to hearing direction from God?

Choose to humbly put someone else's interests before your own today. If you find you have to make a concerted effort to do this, bring this fact to the Lord and ask for His help.

Day 5

Read Psalm 37:7–9. Why do you think the psalmist says followers of God don't have to fret when evil people succeed in their plans—but instead just wait on the Lord?

Sometimes patience isn't so much about waiting as it is about refraining from angry retaliation when someone offends you. What happens if you give in to this type of anger (see verse 8)?

What do you typically do when you're angry? How can you better "turn from wrath" (verse 8) in those times?

_____

_____

_____

_____

If you're not aware of your anger, ask God to make you aware of it today. If you are all too aware of it, ask Him to work inside you so you can begin to get your temper under control.

FOLLOWING GOD
BY *SHUNNING*
WORLDLY WISDOM

CONSIDER IT

We know from the very first chapter in the Bible that God alone is the Creator of everything. Satan creates nothing—his only power is to bend or counterfeit what God has created. He does this often, however, so we shouldn't be surprised that just as there is "godly wisdom" that originates in the Lord and leads to a flourishing life, so there is a "worldly wisdom" that attempts to make life work apart from God—but ultimately fails. You may have encountered this type of wisdom in a university or in the media. It's everywhere.

The Bible repeatedly commends true wisdom. It also resolutely warns against the distorted and counterfeit wisdom that is not from God. We need to learn the difference in order to reject the world's promises and enticements regarding "the good life." Jesus alone offers abundant life for those who believe—the world cannot duplicate this. We also must not allow bad experiences with false wisdom to turn us away from true wisdom. To settle for the immaturity and ignorance of worldly wisdom would be like giving up on money after a bad experience with counterfeit bills!

In this session, we'll learn to identify each type of wisdom and discern one from the other. To know what constitutes false wisdom can sharpen our eye for the fake and heighten our valuation of the real.

1. *Have you ever had contact with a type of wisdom that you now recognize as false? If so, describe your experience.*

---

2. *How has your experience with false wisdom affected your openness toward true wisdom? What is the problem in not distinguishing the two kinds of wisdom?*

Experience It

Trust in *My unfailing Love*—thanking Me for the good you do not see. When evil seems to be flourishing in the world around you, it can look as if things are spinning out of control. But rest assured: I'm not wringing My hands helplessly, wondering what to do next. I am still in control, and there is behind-the-scenes goodness in the midst of the turmoil. So I urge you to thank Me not only for the blessings you can see but for the ones you cannot see.

My *wisdom and knowledge* are deeper and richer than words can express. *My judgments are unsearchable, and My paths beyond tracing out!* This is why trusting Me *at all times* is so crucial. You must not let confusing circumstances shake your faith in Me. When your world feels unsteady, the disciplines of trusting and thanking Me serve to stabilize you. Remember: *I am always with you. I guide you with My counsel, and afterward I will take you into Glory.* Let this hidden treasure—your heavenly inheritance—lead you into joyous thanksgiving!

—From *Jesus Always*, October 18

3. *In 1 John 4:4, we read that "the one who is in [a believer in Christ] is greater than the one who is in the world." Why is it crucial to know that God is not helpless in the presence of evil?*

4. *What, if anything, do you find confusing about your present circumstances? How are you dealing with the situation?*

When the way just ahead of you seems too difficult, turn to Me and say: "I can't, but *we* (You and I together) *can.*" Acknowledging your inability to handle things on your own is a healthy dose of reality. However, this is only one part of the equation, because a sense of inadequacy by itself can be immobilizing. The most important part of the equation is recognizing My abiding Presence with you and My desire to help you.

Pour out your heart to Me. Ask Me to carry your burdens and show you the way forward. Don't waste energy worrying about things that are beyond your control. Instead, use that energy to connect with Me. *Seek My Face continually.* Be ready to follow wherever I lead, trusting Me to open up the way before you as you go.

Dare to see your inadequacy as a door to My Presence. View your journey as an adventure that you share with Me. Remain in close communication with Me, enjoying My company as we journey together.

—From *Jesus Always*, May 23

5. *If you are a Christian, what are some ways to become more aware of God's abiding presence with you and His desire to help you?*

_____

_____

_____

_____

6. *Have you been asking God to show you the way forward? If so, what has been the result?*

_____

_____

_____

_____

STUDY IT

Read aloud the following passages from James 3:13–18 and 4:13–17. Each of these passages contrasts true wisdom with the counterfeit wisdom of the world. As you read, note that—just as you've already seen in Proverbs—James associates true wisdom with humility. Humility isn't thinking badly of yourself; it's thinking about yourself less than you think about God and others. It's the transfer of attention away from the self. The word translated as "submissive" in James 3:17 means being willing to listen and open to reason. The second passage, 4:13–17, is an example of the contrast between humble wisdom and arrogant "wisdom."

[3:13] Who is wise and understanding among you? Let them show it by their good life, by deeds done in the humility that comes from wisdom. [14] But if you harbor bitter envy and selfish ambition in your hearts, do not boast about it or deny the truth. [15] Such "wisdom" does not come down from heaven but is earthly, unspiritual, demonic. [16] For where you have envy and selfish ambition, there you find disorder and every evil practice. [17] But the wisdom that comes from heaven is first of all pure; then peace-loving, considerate, submissive, full of mercy and good fruit, impartial and sincere. [18] Peacemakers who sow in peace reap a harvest of righteousness.

[4:13] Now listen, you who say, "Today or tomorrow we will go to this or that city, spend a year there, carry on business and make money." [14] Why, you do not even know what will happen tomorrow. What is your life? You are a mist that appears for a little while and then vanishes. [15] Instead, you ought to say, "If it is the Lord's will, we will live and do this or that." [16] As it is, you boast in your arrogant schemes. All such boasting is evil. [17] If anyone, then, knows the good they ought to do and doesn't do it, it is sin for them.

7. *What are the signposts of earthly wisdom? How would you express these in your own words?*

---

8. *Why is it critical to be aware of the allure of earthly wisdom when seeking God's direction?*

---

9. *Choose one of the qualities of "the wisdom that comes from heaven" (James 3:17). Why is this quality important for you to possess as you seek God's direction for your life?*

---

10. *Now look at some of the qualities of worldly wisdom mentioned in James 4:13. What is the problem with following this kind of "wisdom"?*

---

11. *How would you describe the inner attitude of someone who says, "If it is the Lord's will, we will live and do this or that" (4:15)?*

_____

_____

_____

_____

12. *Take two minutes of silence to reread the passage, looking for a sentence, phrase, or even one word that stands out as something Jesus may want you to focus on in your life. If you're meeting with a group, the leader will keep track of time. At the end of two minutes, you may share with the group the word or phrase that came to you in the silence.*

_____

_____

_____

_____

13. *Read the passage aloud again. Take another two minutes of silence, prayerfully considering what response God might want you to make to what you have read in His Word. If you're meeting with a group, the leader will again keep track of time. At the end of two minutes, you may share with the group what came to you in the silence if you wish.*

_____

_____

_____

14. *If you're meeting with a group, how can the members pray for you? If you're using this study on your own, what would you like to say to God right now?*

LIVE IT

This week's readings are focused on some of the "mockers" or "fools" who are portrayed in the book of Proverbs. Read each passage slowly, pausing to think about what is being said. Rather than approaching this as an assignment to complete, think of it as an opportunity to meet with the One who loves you most. Use any of the questions that are helpful.

Day 1

Read Proverbs 14:6. Why do you think the mocker seeks wisdom but finds none?

What does it mean to be discerning?

When have you seen a mocker in action? How did he or she treat God's wisdom?

Ask God to reveal if you have any qualities of the mocker.

Day 2

Read Proverbs 19:20–21. In the book of Proverbs, an "unwise" person is anyone who is only interested in worldly wisdom—those who think of themselves as clever but, in fact, ignore true wisdom from God. How does accepting God's wisdom lead to becoming wise?

What happens when people try to follow their own "wise" ways without involving God?

Do you tend to be open to receiving godly advice and discipline from those in authority over you? What problems, if any, have you had with this in the past?

Pray that God will help you faithfully respond to godly correction throughout the day.

Day 3

Read Proverbs 21:24. What qualities does this verse ascribe to the mocker?

_____

_____

_____

_____

How do these qualities fit with what you've already learned about earthly wisdom?

_____

_____

_____

_____

Why does pride often lead to uncontrolled anger? What's the connection?

_____

_____

_____

_____

Pay attention to your temper today. If you are prone to anger, offer it up to God and seek His guidance.

Day 4

Read Proverbs 22:10. Think of someone you know who causes strife. Does that person have the qualities of a mocker?

_____

_____

_____

Why do you think this proverb speaks of separating yourself from the presence of mockers rather than trying to change them?

_____

_____

What is the best way you know to deal with the mocker in your life? Does getting mad help? Why or why not?

_____

_____

_____

Let God show you how to deal effectively with any mockers in your life.

Day 5

Read Psalm 1:1–2. How does this psalm suggest you should respond to mockers?

_____

_____

_____

Why does this response make sense?

_____

_____

_____

_____

What can you do if you are unable to avoid a mocker? (Consider Matthew 5:33–35.)

_____

_____

_____

_____

Pray for protection from mockers today . . . and also for the strength to love them.

FOLLOWING GOD BY LOVING HIS WORD

CONSIDER IT

If you want to know what people value, just look at how they spend their time and money. Many folks, for example, have no problem paying eight hundred dollars for a phone, either all at once or in installments. They do this because they value what the phone enables them to do.

Compare that to the amount of time the average person spends each day searching God's Word for wisdom, or the money they spend on Bibles and resources that help them know God and His Word. For most people, phones top Bibles in both arenas.

In this session, we will look at the incomparable value God's Word offers us for directing our lives. We'll consider its straightforward instructions (*do more of this and none of that*), in addition to the guidance we receive from learning how God dealt with various situations described in the story portions of the Bible. Most of us know it would be good for us to spend more time in God's Word, and this session will be a motivator.

1. *What have you gotten out of the "Live It" daily Bible reflection times in this study, or from whatever other habit of Bible reading you have?*

_____

_____

_____

_____

2. *What helps you spend time in God's Word? What gets in the way?*

_____

_____

_____

_____

EXPERIENCE IT

I am making you *new in the attitude of your mind*. Living close to Me is all about newness and change. I am transforming you *by the entire renewal of your mind*. This is a massive undertaking; you will be under construction till the day you die. However, unlike the inanimate materials that builders use to construct houses, *you* are living, breathing "material." I have given you the amazing ability to think things out and make important choices. I want you to use this godlike ability to cooperate with Me as I transform you. This involves *putting off your old self*—your old way of thinking and doing things—and *putting on the new self*.

To make good, godly choices, you need to know Me as I truly am. Search for Me in My Word; ask My Spirit to illuminate it—shining His Light so that Scripture comes alive to you. The more you choose to live according to My will, the more you will become *like Me*, and the more you can enjoy *walking in the Light of My Presence*.

—FROM *JESUS ALWAYS*, JUNE 24

3. *You may want direct instructions on what to do, but instead God often asks His children to rely on a gift that He has given them: the ability to think things out and make important choices with the guidance of His Holy Spirit. How much do you value this gift? Why?*

----

4. *According to this reading, how does God's Word help you make good choices? Can you think of some additional ways it aids your decision making?*

Stop judging by mere appearances, and make a right judgment. I made this statement at the temple in Jerusalem, teaching that judging can be either good or bad. I was speaking to people who had assessed Me on the basis of appearances: focusing on the letter of the Law rather than the spirit of the Law. What they were doing was wrong, but that doesn't mean *all* judgments are wrong. I forbid superficial, self-righteous, and hypocritical evaluations. But I do want My followers to make *righteous* assessments about moral and theological issues—based on biblical truth.

In this age of "tolerance," there is immense pressure on people to refrain from making statements that differentiate right from wrong. The fear of being labeled "intolerant" has silenced many people who know how to make right judgments. I want you to have the courage to *speak the truth in love* as I lead you to do so. The best preparation is to search the Scriptures and your heart. Then ask My Spirit to speak through you even as He loves others through you.

—From *Jesus Always*, May 13

5. *When has God's Word helped you make a right judgment about something?*

6. *What is an example from your life about judging by appearances—either when someone judged you in this way, or you judged someone else?*

STUDY IT

Read aloud the following passage from Psalm 119:97–105. This entire psalm is an acrostic poem, which means the first eight verses all begin with the first letter of the Hebrew alphabet, the next eight begin with the second letter, and so on, through the whole alphabet. In verses that repeat and amplify one another, the poem celebrates the speaker's love for the Word of God.

Like James, this psalmist is more interested in obeying what the Word says to do. When he speaks of meditating on the statutes, he means thinking deeply and closely about what they mean and how they can best be lived.

[97] Oh, how I love your law!
   I meditate on it all day long.

[98] Your commands are always with me
      and make me wiser than my enemies.

[99] I have more insight than all my teachers,
      for I meditate on your statutes.

[100] I have more understanding than the elders,
      for I obey your precepts.

[101] I have kept my feet from every evil path
      so that I might obey your word.

[102] I have not departed from your laws,
      for you yourself have taught me.

[103] How sweet are your words to my taste,
      sweeter than honey to my mouth!

[104] I gain understanding from your precepts;
      therefore I hate every wrong path.

[105] Your word is a lamp for my feet,
      a light on my path.

7. *What does it mean to love God's law (see verse 97)? Why do you think the psalmist felt this way?*

_____

_____

_____

8. *Consider Jesus' teaching in the Sermon on the Mount (Matthew 5–7). What would be the value of meditating on these words as guidance from Him on how to live?*

_____

_____

_____

_____

9. *How could you meditate on God's statutes?*

_____

_____

_____

10. *Given that God's instructions are often challenging, how can we honestly say, "How sweet are your words to my taste, sweeter than honey to my mouth" (verse 103)?*

_____

_____

_____

_____

11. *When was a time that God's Word was a lamp for your feet and a light on your path (see verse 105)?*

_____

_____

_____

12. *Take two minutes of silence to reread the passage, looking for a sentence, phrase, or even one word that stands out as something Jesus may want you to focus on in your life. If you're meeting with a group, the leader will keep track of time. At the end of two minutes, you may share with the group the word or phrase that came to you in the silence.*

_____

_____

_____

13. *Read the passage aloud again. Take another two minutes of silence, prayerfully considering what response God might want you to make to what you have read in His Word. If you're meeting with a group, the leader will again keep track of time. At the end of two minutes, you may share with the group what came to you in the silence if you wish.*

_____

_____

_____

14. *If you're meeting with a group, how can the members pray for you? If you're using this study on your own, what would you like to say to God right now?*

Live It

This week's readings are focused on Jesus' teachings in the Sermon on the Mount that provide guidance for how His followers are to live. Read each passage slowly, pausing to think about what is being said. Rather than approaching this as an assignment to complete, think of it as an opportunity to meet with the One who loves you most. Use any of the questions that are helpful.

Day 1

Read Matthew 5:13. In the ancient world, salt was prized as a flavoring and a preservative. What do you think it means for Christians to be the "salt of the earth"?

If you are a Christian, how could you be the salt of the earth in your corner of the world?

How can God help you be the salt of the earth?

_____

_____

_____

Look today for an opportunity to bring out the best in someone.

Day 2

Read Matthew 5:14–16. What do you think it means for Christians to be the light of the world ?

_____

_____

_____

If you are a Christian, how could you be the light of the world where you live?

_____

_____

_____

What help do you need in being the light of the world?

_____

_____

_____

Be on the lookout for a chance to treat someone with compassion in this day.

Day 3

Read Matthew 5:21–22. Why do you think Jesus puts anger on the same level as murder?

Are outbursts of anger a problem for you? If so, where do you think they come from?

If outbursts are not a problem for you, do you nurse resentments silently, or are you just not usually an angry person? Explain.

Today, pay attention to any moments when you feel anger, frustration, resentment, or any of their "cousins." Watch what you tend to do with those feelings.

Day 4

Read Matthew 5:38–42. How would you summarize in your own words the stance toward other people that Jesus instructs His followers to have?

Most people have a hard time living like this. Why do you think that's the case?

Why is this a better way to live than retaliating for every offense?

Seek God's help so that you may respond to offense with kindness today.

Day 5

Read Matthew 5:43–47. How do you suppose it's possible to love your enemies?

Jesus wasn't naive about enemies. He had them—and they even plotted His execution. What rationale does He give for loving one's enemies in this passage?

As you look back on this week of getting direction from the Scriptures on how to live, what insight stands out to you?

Look for ways to actively love those who aren't always nice to you.

FOLLOWING GOD BY LISTENING TO THE SPIRIT OF TRUTH

CONSIDER IT

We often want God's direction in planning our next major steps in life: *Should I take this job? Should I marry this person? Which church should I join?* We want God to provide His direction within our agenda. However, God invites us to receive *His* direction within *His* agenda. This is why He sends His Holy Spirit to dwell within the heart of every believer.

For those of us who are Christians, we can think of the Holy Spirit as our counselor and advocate (see Isaiah 11:2). The world often tells us to travel down the path that it deems best—what Jesus called the broad road "that leads to destruction" (Matthew 7:13)—but the Holy Spirit intervenes and guides God's children back on the path that the Lord has set for us. The Holy Spirit empowers us to speak what He knows needs to be said and do what He knows needs to be done. The Holy Spirit can even help us lead others off the path to destruction and to the road of life.

This session is the first of two in which we will explore the guidance of the Holy Spirit. As we will discuss, Jesus called the Holy Spirit "the Spirit of truth," and when He enters into the lives of God's children, He provides wisdom to help them discern the foolishness of the world and walk in God's will. As Paul wrote, "The Spirit helps us in our weakness. We do not know what we ought to pray for, but the Spirit himself intercedes for us" (Romans 8:26).

1. *Up to this point in time, what has been your perception or mental picture of the Holy Spirit?*

_____

_____

_____

_____

2. *How do you respond to the idea that the Holy Spirit is your guide in a world that desires to lead you away from the things of God? What are the implications of this for your life?*

EXPERIENCE IT

The Christian life is all about trusting Me: in good times *and* in hard times. I am Lord over all your circumstances, so I want to be involved in every aspect of your life. You can quickly connect with Me by affirming your confidence in Me here and now. When your world seems dark and you trust Me anyway, My Light shines brightly through you. Your display of transcendent faith weakens spiritual forces of evil. And My supernatural Light showing through you blesses and strengthens people around you.

Clinging to Me in the dark requires you to persistently exert your willpower. But while you're grasping onto Me, remember: My hand has an eternal grip on yours—I will never let go of you! Moreover, My Spirit helps you keep hanging on. When you feel on the verge of giving up, cry out for His assistance: "Help me, Holy Spirit!" This brief prayer enables you to tap into His limitless resources. Even when your circumstances look dark and threatening, My Light is still *shining on* in surpassing splendor!

—FROM *JESUS ALWAYS*, JANUARY 15

3. *How can followers of Christ go about affirming their confidence in God here and now?*

4. *Have you ever cried out (aloud or silently), "Help me, Holy Spirit"? If so, what happened? If not, what has kept you from doing that?*

_____

_____

_____

When the task before you looks daunting, refuse to be intimidated. Discipline your thinking to view the challenge as a privilege rather than a burdensome duty. Make the effort to replace your "I have to" mentality with an "I get to" approach. This will make all the difference in your perspective—transforming drudgery into delight. This is not a magic trick; the work still has to be done. But the change in your viewpoint can help you face the challenging chore joyfully and confidently.

As you go about your work, perseverance is essential. If you start to grow weary or discouraged, remind yourself: "I *get* to do this!" Then thank Me for giving you the ability and strength to do what needs to be done. Thankfulness clears your mind and draws you close to Me. Remember that My Spirit who lives in you is *the Helper*; ask Him to help you when you're perplexed. As you ponder problems and seek solutions, He will guide your mind. *Whatever you do, work at it with all your heart—as working for Me.*

—From *Jesus Always*, October 20

5. *In Colossians 3:23, Paul says, "Whatever you do, work at it with all your heart, as working for the Lord, not for human masters." Why is it better to see your work in terms of something you "get" to do rather than something you "have" to do? How easy is this shift for you?*

_____

_____

_____

6. *What do you think Jesus meant when He referred to the Holy Spirit as our advocate or helper (see John 15:26)?*

_____

_____

_____

STUDY IT

Read aloud the following passages from John 14:26 and 16:12–15. Jesus is giving a discourse to prepare His disciples for His bodily departure from the world. He promises that instead of being physically present with them, He is going to send the Holy Spirit—which will actually be better for them in the long term. The word translated "advocate" in John 14:26 was used in the ancient world for a lawyer who stood up for someone in court and offered legal counsel. The Advocate, the Holy Spirit, offers wisdom, the right words, support, and strength to those who choose to follow Christ.

> 14:26 "But the Advocate, the Holy Spirit, whom the Father will send in my name, will teach you all things and will remind you of everything I have said to you."
>
> 16:12 "I have much more to say to you, more than you can now bear. 13 But when he, the Spirit of truth, comes, he will guide you into all the truth. He will not speak on his own; he will speak only what he hears, and he will tell you what is yet to come. 14 He will glorify me because it is from me that he will receive what he will make known to you. 15 All that belongs to the Father is mine. That is why I said the Spirit will receive from me what he will make known to you."

7. *What do you learn in John 14:26 about the Spirit's guidance?*

_____

_____

_____

8. *Think about what you've learned the word "advocate" means in this verse. For what current circumstances do you need the Holy Spirit to come alongside you as your advocate?*

_____

_____

_____

9. *Why is it significant that Jesus calls the Holy Spirit "the Spirit of truth" (John 16:13)?*

_____

_____

_____

10. *How does the Holy Spirit guide God's sons and daughters into all truth?*

_____

_____

_____

11. *Why do you think it is important that the Spirit communicates only and exactly what comes from God the Father and Jesus (see 16:13–14)?*

_____

_____

_____

12. *Take two minutes of silence to reread the passage, looking for a sentence, phrase, or even one word that stands out as something Jesus may want you to focus on in your life. If you're meeting with a group, the leader will keep track* *of time. At the end of two minutes, you may share with the group the word or phrase that came to you in the silence.*

---

13. *Read the passage aloud again. Take another two minutes of silence, prayerfully considering what response God might want you to make to what you have read in His Word. If you're meeting with a group, the leader will again keep track of time. At the end of two minutes, you may share with the group what came to you in the silence if you wish.*

---

14. *If you're meeting with a group, how can the members pray for you? If you're using this study on your own, what would you like to say to God right now?*

LIVE IT

This week's readings are focused on the theme of how the Holy Spirit guides the lives of Jesus' followers. Read each passage slowly, pausing to think about what is being said. Rather than approaching this as an assignment to complete, think of it as an opportunity to meet with the One who loves you most. Use any of the questions that are helpful.

Day 1

Read John 14:15–18. What connection does Jesus make between loving Him, obeying Him, and receiving the Holy Spirit?

Why do you think obedience is so important for Christians?

Do you ever feel that Jesus has left you as an orphan? What reassurance does the promise of the Holy Spirit offer you if you are a believer?

Look for a chance today to obey the words and example of Jesus.

Day 2

Read John 15:26–27. What does this passage say the Holy Spirit will do?

In what ways did Jesus' disciples testify about Him?

In what ways do you testify about Jesus? How can the Holy Spirit help you with this if you're a follower of Christ?

Watch for a chance today to testify about Jesus. Ask the Holy Spirit to help you be a witness for Christ if you've accepted Him as your Lord and Savior.

Day 3

Read Psalm 51:10–12. In this passage, David refers to the presence of the Holy Spirit in his life. Why is it important to know the Holy Spirit was active in Old Testament times as well?

What does the psalmist say about his own spirit? About the Holy Spirit?

_____

_____

_____

_____

Why would it be terrible if God disciplined His children by taking away His Holy Spirit?

_____

_____

_____

_____

Pray for God to give you a steadfast spirit today that listens closely to the Holy Spirit.

Day 4

Read Mark 13:9–11. Jesus is speaking to His disciples in this passage. How did His words apply to them in their generation?

_____

_____

_____

_____

How do His words apply to God's children in this generation?

Have you ever had an experience when you knew the Holy Spirit was guiding you about what to say? Explain.

If you are a follower of Christ, ask the Holy Spirit to give you the words to say in any situation where you may need them in this day.

Day 5

Read Luke 11:11–13. What does this passage say about the type of gifts that God provides to His children? How does this relate to the gift of the Holy Spirit?

If you are a follower of Christ, are you in the habit of asking the Father to fill you with the Holy Spirit? Why or why not?

_____

_____

_____

_____

Why do you suppose the Holy Spirit is a more valuable gift than anything else a Christian might ask for from the Father?

_____

_____

_____

_____

Cry out to God today to fill you with the Holy Spirit so you may speak about Jesus and to do the things that He wants you to do.

FOLLOWING GOD BY OBEYING THE HOLY SPIRIT'S PROMPTINGS

Consider It

Like a good parent, God directs His followers' path by helping them grow in wisdom so they can learn to make wise decisions. He has given us the Bible, which is full of principles and examples to guide us onto wise paths. He has provided other believers in Christ, who can give us wise counsel. Yet even with all this help, we have a great deal of freedom in making our own choices.

Still, a good parent also gives his children specific instructions: *Do this; don't do that.* God does the same. The Holy Spirit lives inside every Christian, and He prompts believers to act in certain ways so they stay in step with Him. These instructions are outworkings of the principles God has given in the Bible—and they never contradict the Scriptures.

In this session, we'll consider how this prompting of the Holy Spirit works in the life of a believer, and we'll think about how often we should expect to receive this kind of guidance if we belong to God. We'll also explore how to make ourselves available to hear the Spirit when He speaks.

1. *By the time you were a teenager, how often did your parents give you direct instructions on what to do throughout your day?*

2. *If you are a Christian, when was the last time you received a prompting from the Holy Spirit to do something? How did you know it was Him?*

Experience It

One of My names is *Wonderful Counselor*. I understand you far, far better than you understand yourself. So come to *Me* with your problems and insecurities, seeking My counsel. In the Light of My loving Presence you can see yourself as you really are: radiantly lovely in My brilliant righteousness. Though My righteousness is perfect, you will continue to struggle with imperfections—yours and others'—as long as you live in this world. Still, your standing with Me is secure. *Nothing in all creation can separate you from My Love!*

A good counselor helps you recognize truth and live according to it. *Actually, I was born and came into the world to testify to the truth.* So be open and honest when you bring Me your concerns. Also, fill your mind and heart with My Word, which contains absolute truth.

A *wonderful* counselor is not only extremely good at helping people but also able to inspire delight or pleasure. *Delight yourself in Me*, beloved, *and I will give you the desires of your heart.*

—From *Jesus Always*, February 22

3. *Describe a time when you needed God as your Wonderful Counselor. Did you listen to Him when He spoke to you?*

_____

_____

_____

4. *How has God helped you recognize the truth and live by it in your faith journey? How do you go about making yourself available for Him to do this?*

_____

_____

_____

Your competence comes from Me. This means there is no place for pride in your achievements. It also means you are capable of much more than you think possible. The combination of your natural abilities and My supernatural empowerment is very effective. I have called you to live in joyful dependence on Me, so don't hesitate to ask Me for help. Make every effort to discern My will for you—searching the Scriptures and *seeking My Face.* Also, seek wise counsel from other Christians. I will show you the way to go forward according to My wisdom and will.

Ask My Spirit to guide you along the pathway I have chosen for you. This Holy Helper will equip and empower you to achieve My purposes in your life. Thank Me for everything: the abilities I have given you, the opportunities before you, and My Spirit's enabling you to accomplish important things in My kingdom. Stay in communication with Me, enjoying My Company as you journey along *the path of Life. In My Presence is fullness of Joy*!

—FROM *JESUS ALWAYS*, JULY 11

5. *Which of the following do you rely on most often as you seek to discern God's will? Which do you rely on less? Why?*
- ☐ Searching the Scriptures
- ☐ Seeking God in prayer
- ☐ Seeking wise counsel from other Christians
- ☐ Other (specify):

6. *When you ask the Holy Spirit to guide you, what usually happens? Do you receive guidance, or do you feel like you're just getting silence?*

STUDY IT

Read aloud the following passage from Acts 16:6–15. This passage picks up in the middle of an account of the apostle Paul's missionary journey through what is now Turkey. Paul wanted to continue to minister there, but the Holy Spirit blocked him in some way. It appears that this went on for a considerable period of time—perhaps weeks or months. Paul then received the divine call to go to Macedonia, which is part of modern-day Greece. Paul had not yet taken the message about Jesus that far west. In verse 10, Luke, the writer of this book, begins to speak of "we," so it appears he joined Paul's traveling team just as they were setting out for Macedonia.

6 Paul and his companions traveled throughout the region of Phrygia and Galatia, having been kept by the Holy Spirit from preaching the word in the province of Asia. 7 When they came to the border of Mysia, they tried to enter Bithynia, but the Spirit of Jesus would not allow them to. 8 So they passed by Mysia and went down to Troas. 9 During the night Paul had a vision of a man of Macedonia standing and begging him, "Come over to Macedonia and help us." 10 After Paul had seen the vision, we got ready at once to leave for Macedonia, concluding that God had called us to preach the gospel to them.

11 From Troas we put out to sea and sailed straight for Samothrace, and the next day we went on to Neapolis. 12 From there we traveled to Philippi, a Roman colony and the leading city of that district of Macedonia. And we stayed there several days.

13 On the Sabbath we went outside the city gate to the river, where we expected to find a place of prayer. We sat down and began to speak to the women who had gathered there.14 One of those listening was a woman from the city of Thyatira named Lydia, a dealer in purple cloth. She was a worshiper of God. The Lord opened her heart to respond to Paul's message. 15 When she and the members of her household were baptized, she invited us to her home. "If you consider me a believer in the Lord," she said, "come and stay at my house." And she persuaded us.

7. *How did Paul and his companions respond when the Holy Spirit prevented them from preaching in the province of Asia (see verse 6)?*

_____

_____

_____

8. *What do you make of the fact that Luke speaks of the Holy Spirit in verse 6 and the Spirit of Jesus in verse 7? What do you learn about God from this?*

_____

_____

_____

9. *Why do you think the Holy Spirit spoke to Paul in a vision rather than just prompting him in his heart to go to Macedonia?*

_____

_____

_____

_____

10. *Have you ever had your plan blocked for a period of time and had to wait on God for direction? If so, what happened? How well did you respond to this setback?*

_____

_____

_____

_____

11. *When Paul and his team arrived in Philippi, the Lord led them to a woman named Lydia, who was receptive to their message and accepted Christ as her Savior (see verses 11–15). If you are a Christian, how has the Holy Spirit likewise led you to serve and help those in need?*

12. *Take two minutes of silence to reread the passage, looking for a sentence, phrase, or even one word that stands out as something Jesus may want you to focus on in your life. If you're meeting with a group, the leader will keep track of time. At the end of two minutes, you may share with the group the word or phrase that came to you in the silence.*

13. *Read the passage aloud again. Take another two minutes of silence, prayerfully considering what response God might want you to make to what you have read in His Word. If you're meeting with a group, the leader will again keep track of time. At the end of two minutes, you may share with the group what came to you in the silence if you wish.*

14. *If you're meeting with a group, how can the members pray for you? If you're using this study on your own, what would you like to say to God right now?*

LIVE IT

This week's readings are focused on God's guidance as provided to the early church in the book of Acts. Read each passage slowly, pausing to think about what is being said. Rather than approaching this as an assignment to complete, think of it as an opportunity to meet with the One who loves you most. Use any of the questions that are helpful.

Day 1

Read Acts 8:26–30. How does Philip receive guidance in this passage?

Ethiopia was at the southern edge of the known world at this time. Why do you think God went to such trouble to be sure that this man heard about Jesus? What does this say about God?

What place does evangelism have in the life of a believer? If the Holy Spirit asked you to talk with a nonbeliever about Jesus, how would you respond?

Be ready to follow God's lead and share your "God story" with someone in need of Him today.

Day 2

Read Acts 9:10–15. How does the Lord direct Ananias in this passage?

What reservations did Ananias have about following God's directions?

Has the Lord ever directed you to take a big risk on His behalf? If yes, what did you do? If no, what do you think you would do in Ananias's position?

Watch for a chance today to take a risk on God's behalf.

Day 3

Read Acts 10:1–6. How does God guide Cornelius in this passage?

Cornelius was not a Jew, but he and his household were attracted to the one true God. What do you think God was trying to accomplish by giving Cornelius specific instructions about a man in another town whom he had never met?

As you read these instances of visions and angelic visitations in Acts, what pattern can you see emerging that you can apply in your own journey with God?

Ask God to help you obey His promptings, whether they're clear and specific or delivered in a more subtle manner.

Day 4

Read Acts 10:9–20. How does God get Peter's attention in this passage?

Up to this point, Peter and the other disciples hadn't really considered that God might want to spread the news about Jesus to non-Jews. How does that help you understand the point of God's dramatic means of communication in this chapter in Acts?

Has God ever asked you to change direction? If so, how did He communicate with you about it? If not, what would it take for you to make a significant change in the life you're living now?

Give God permission today to radically change your direction or your perspective.

Day 5

Read Acts 11:19–29. Recount the situation in the early church when this passage opens.

How is Barnabas described in verse 24? What do you think this means?

What do you learn about the ministry of a prophet from this passage? What was the immediate result of Agabus's prophecy through the Holy Spirit?

Thank God today for what you have learned in this study about how He wants to direct you. Tell Him you're entirely willing to let Him train you and guide you.

LEADER'S NOTES

Thank you for your willingness to lead a group through this *Jesus Always* study. The rewards of leading are different from the rewards of participating, and we hope you find your own walk with Jesus deepened by this experience. In many ways, your group meeting will be structured like other Bible studies in which you've participated. You'll want to open in prayer, for example, and ask people to silence their phones. These leader's notes will focus on elements of the study that may be new to you.

CONSIDER IT

This first portion of the study functions as an icebreaker. It gets the group members thinking about the topic at hand by asking them to share from their own experience. Some people may be tempted to tell a long story in response to one of these questions, but the goal is to keep the answers brief. Ideally, you want everyone in the group to have a chance to answer the *Consider It* questions, so you may want to say up front that everyone needs to limit his or her answer to one minute.

With the rest of the study, it is generally not a good idea to go around the circle and have everyone answer every question—a free-flowing discussion is more desirable. But with the *Consider It* questions, you can go around the circle. Encourage shy people to share, but don't force them. Tell the group they should feel free to pass if they prefer not to answer a question.

EXPERIENCE IT

This is the group's chance to talk about excerpts from the *Jesus Always* devotional. You will need to monitor this discussion closely so that you have enough time for the actual study of God's Word that follows. If the group has a long and rich discussion on one of the devotional excerpts, you may choose to skip the other one and move on to the Bible study. Don't feel obliged to cover every *Experience It* question if the conversation is fruitful. On the other hand, do move on if the group gets off on a tangent.

STUDY IT

Try to do the *Study It* exercise in session 1 on your own before the group meets the first time so you can coach people on what to expect. Note that this section may be a little different from Bible studies your group has done in the past. The group will talk about the Bible passage as usual, but then there will be several minutes of silence so individuals can pray about what God might want to say to them personally through the reading. It will be up to you to keep track of the time and call people back to the discussion when the time is up. (There are some good timer apps that play a gentle chime or other pleasant sound instead of a disruptive noise.) If members aren't used to being silent in a group, brief them on what to expect.

Don't be afraid to let people sit in silence. Two minutes of quiet may seem like a long time at first, but it will help to train group members to sit in silence with God when they are alone. They can remain where they are in the circle, or if you have space, you can let them go off by themselves to other rooms at your instruction. If your group meets in a home, ask the host before the meeting which rooms are available for use. Some people will be more comfortable in the quiet if they have a bit of space from others.

When the group reconvenes after the time of silence, invite them to share what they experienced. There are several questions provided in this study guide that you can ask. Note that it's not necessary to cover every question if the group has a good discussion going. It's also not necessary to go around the circle and make everyone share.

Don't be concerned if the group members are reserved and slow to share after the exercise. People are often quiet when they are pulling together their ideas, and the exercise will have been a new experience for many of them. Just ask a question and let it hang in the air until someone speaks up. You can then say, "Thank you. What about others? What came to you when you sat with the passage?"

Some people may say they found it hard to quiet their minds enough to focus on the passage for those few minutes. Tell them this is okay. They are practicing a skill, and sometimes skills take time to learn. If they learn to sit quietly with God's Word in a group, they will become much more comfortable sitting with the Word on their own. Remind them that spending time in the Bible each day is one of the most valuable things they can do as believers in Christ.

PREPARATION

It's not necessary for group members to prepare anything for the study ahead of time. However, at the end of each study are five days' worth of suggestions for spending time in God's Word during the next week. These daily times are optional but valuable, so encourage the group to do them. Also, invite them to bring their questions and insights to the group at your next meeting, especially if they had a breakthrough moment or if they didn't understand something.

As the leader, there are a few things you should do to prepare for each meeting:

- *Read through the session.* This will help you become familiar with the content and know how to structure the discussion times.

- *Spend five to ten minutes doing the* Study It *questions on your own.* When the group meets, you'll be watching the clock, so you'll probably have a more fulfilling time with the passage if you do the exercise ahead of time. You can then spend time in the passage again with the group. This way, you'll be sure to have the key verses for that session deeply in your mind.

- *Pray for your group.* Pray especially that God will guide them in how to embrace the love that Jesus has demonstrated for them and, in turn, share that love with others in their world who need to experience it.

- *Bring extra supplies to your meeting.* Group members should bring their own pens for writing notes on the Bible reflection, but it is a good idea to have extras available for those who forget. You may also want to bring paper and Bibles for those who may have neglected to bring their study guides to the meeting.

Below you will find suggested answers for some of the study questions. Note that in many cases there is no one right answer, especially when the group members are sharing their personal experiences.

Session 1: Following God by Treasuring His Wisdom

1. *Answers will vary, but some good examples include the internet, television, magazines, books, the people with whom we interact, billboards, road signs, food labels, and our five senses.*

2. *Of course, not all information is bad—there's just a lot to sift through. The problem for most of us is that we are so buried in information each and every day that we have trouble focusing on what is truly valuable from an eternal perspective. It's all so "noisy" that discerning the voice of God in the jumble can be difficult.*

3. *When we say that God is our treasure or great reward, it means that we value Him above all other things in our lives. It means that we've placed our hopes for a fulfilling life on this earth (and eternal life after our time on this world is over) in Him, willingly following what He commands and trusting in His promises. We understand that the blessings God provides through His wisdom and knowledge are beyond anything we will experience on this earth. We also understand that a deeper relationship with Him and understanding of Him is our greatest goal in life.*

4. *Jesus truly knows the best solutions to every problem. Training our minds to go to Him first in prayer will lead to better solutions and will reduce our anxiety. As the apostle Paul wrote, "Be anxious for nothing, but in everything by prayer and supplication, with thanksgiving, let your requests be made known to God" (Philippians 4:6). Letting our minds race on their own will result in more desperate and self-centered responses to our problems.*

5. *Answers will vary. As leader, share a not-so-good decision, perhaps from your youth. Then talk about how God has guided you into greater wisdom in*

your life.

6. *Studying the Bible is of paramount importance, as is staying close to God through designated times of prayer and as you go through your day. It's crucial to "carry" these sources of truth with us on a daily basis, because what people tell us and what we see on the internet or in the media can be wildly off the mark.*

7. *The author of this poem wants the reader to be receptive (accepting) and even aggressive (calling out, crying aloud, searching) in his pursuit of wisdom. He doesn't want his listener to just sit passively and expect wisdom to come to him, but to go out and make an effort to acquire it. Why? Because wisdom is priceless.*

8. *This passage says the Lord gives to the upright, blameless, just, and faithful. The word "blameless" in this regard doesn't mean the redeemed of God are sinless. Rather, it means they are free from accusation in God's eyes because they have trusted in Christ to cleanse them from sin. Christians are faithful to God's commands and promises, and they are committed to pursuing justice and goodness, even if they fall short sometimes. As we follow God's ways, the Lord favors us with wisdom, which in turn helps us to grow in blamelessness.*

9. *Wisdom protects, guards, and saves those who heed it from the ways of wicked people by revealing what are the right and godly things to do and why those ways are better. The passage claims that, generally speaking (though not in every instance in this lifetime), the people who live wisely and do right will flourish, while the plans of those who do wrong will fail. The thoughtful decisions of the wise spare them the consequences of foolishness or evil and help them avoid unnecessary trouble.*

10. *We conduct this invaluable search by reading the Bible and mining its truths for how we are to live. We can also counsel with wise people, asking them* *not only what they think we should do but why and how they do what they do. In their humility, they may be reluctant to give advice, but we can learn a lot from their example. We can also pray persistently for God's perspective and spend time in His presence.*

11. *Biblical wisdom often involves embracing general principles about how to live and prayerfully discerning how to apply them in our circumstances. For example, the Ten Commandments state broad principles about what is right and wrong. The tenth commandment notes that we should never covet something that belongs to someone else (see Exodus 20:17). So, if we find ourselves envying our neighbor's boat or nice house and wishing we had their possessions, we know God has instructed us to pursue a different way of thinking. The goal is to know and understand the principles the Bible teaches so we can properly apply them in specific situations.*

12. *Answers will vary. It's fine for this process to be unfamiliar to the group at first. Be sure to keep track of time.*

13. *Answers will vary. Note that some people may find the silence intimidating at first. Their anxiety might tempt them to fill the air with noise, but it will be helpful for these group members to just take a quiet moment before God. Let them express their discomfort once you're all gathered together again, but make sure it is balanced by those who found the silence strengthening. Helping people become comfortable with this "holy quiet" will serve their private daily times with God in wonderful ways.*

14. *Take as much time as you can to pray for each other. You might have someone write down the prayer requests so you can keep track of answers to prayer.*

Session 2: Following God by Trusting in Him

1. *Answers will vary. Have some fun with this question as you and your group share stories about your love of or frustration with GPS apps.*

2. *Like these map apps, we have to put our faith and trust in God, assured that if we are looking to Him, He is leading us where we need to go. Should we decide to ignore His direction, thinking we know best, we can quickly become lost. A major difference, of course, is that God rarely speaks to us with an audible voice. Christians listen for His guidance while reading the Bible. They also wait for the Holy Spirit's promptings through prayer, circumstances, and the wise people He puts into their lives. God wants His people to develop wisdom rather than expecting step-by-step instructions every time.*

3. *When circumstances don't go our way as believers in Christ, we can be easily tempted to doubt that God is in control. In such cases, we will typically respond to situations with fear rather than wisdom. But if we trust that God is always in control, we can relax—and this allows us to hear His guidance more clearly. Two things that often distract Christians from hearing God's direction are anxiety and discouragement. Trust in God combats both of these.*

4. *Some group members may know what they need to do to "cling to Jesus' hand," and they simply need the courage to do it—courage that comes from staying close to God. Others may be unsure of what they need to do, so clinging to Jesus' hand may mean continually sending up brief prayers: "Please guide me, Lord." "Help me, Holy Spirit."*

5. *Answers will vary. As the group leader, think in advance about a story you can tell fairly briefly, just in case others in the group have trouble coming up with a story to share. For example, how did you know God wanted you to lead this group?*

6. *It's helpful to know whether we're more tempted to run ahead of God or to drag our heels, as this enables us to recognize that inclination in pressing situations and work to resist it.*

7. *Faithfulness is sticking with someone or something. It's staying committed and loyal in a relationship or cause. The world tempts us to put ourselves first and change our commitments when we no longer feel passion for a person* *or an endeavor. But our feelings are unreliable. Faithfulness inspires us to persevere. Though our feelings come and go, God wants us to stand by our promises and not give up.*

8. *The Lord's understanding is so much greater than ours. Our understanding is limited to what we can perceive in our immediate situation, but God understands the big picture of everything that is going on. In light of this, the smartest thing for us to do in a situation may not be the most obvious choice at the time, and the most loving and faithful thing to do may be in conflict with our own limited understanding. Yet that's exactly where faith steps in.*

9. *Being wise in our own eyes means thinking we know what to do. It's an overriding self-confidence that gets in the way of God-confidence. It is an attitude that lacks humility, tempts us to skip the step of asking God what He desires for us, and rushes ahead without waiting on Him for a response. This undermines our trust in God, demonstrating that we have not put our full faith in Him.*

10. *All our income and possessions ultimately come from God. Our hard work is important, but He is the One who supplies us with the skills, the opportunities, and the health to do what we do. There is therefore no paycheck about which we can say, "I earned this on my own; it's mine." It is all God's. We honor His provision by setting aside a portion of our resources for God's work and trusting that He will help us to live adequately on the amount that remains. God will direct the details of our giving, but the basic principle is trusting Him with everything we have.*

11. *Not all suffering in the life of a Christian is discipline from the Lord. Some of it is just the result of living in a fallen world where disease, mistakes, and human selfishness are commonplace. However, sometimes Christians do act wrongly and reap the consequences. When that happens, we can know that God isn't rejecting us. Rather, He is allowing the consequences because He wants us to grow to greater maturity. Responding to God's direction in* *those moments requires us to move toward Him in trust rather than away from Him in hurt.*

12. *Answers will vary.*

13. *Answers will vary.*

14. *Responses will vary.*

Session 3: Following God by Honoring Him

1. *Answers will vary. This question is designed to help participants connect with the idea of fear as a sometimes-positive thing. For example, it's a good idea to fear a forest fire rushing toward us, because it compels us to act and get out of the way. The fear of getting a traffic ticket can also cause us to make the wise choice to slow down on the road.*

2. *Any phobias we have fall into this category, such as fear of heights, fear of crowds, or fear of riding elevators. Many of us also struggle with fears that limit what we can do in the world—fear of failure, fear of embarrassment, fear of what other people will think. This is not the kind of fear we are meant to have when it comes to God. In fact, a healthy fear of God, which includes reverential respect, will help us overcome our fears of worldly things.*

3. *God is delighted when His children, in reverential "fear" and adoration for Him, submit to His will. He blesses His children when that reverence motivates them to choose His attitudes and goals over their own agendas. As we have said, God loves His children and—like any good parent—doesn't want them to be terrified of Him. However, the Lord does want us to take Him seriously, and put Him first and foremost in our lives.*

4. *Answers will vary. An example would be loving someone who doesn't love us back. A goal might be serve someone who steadfastly resists Him as a way of sharing God's love.*

5. *If people are shy about sharing where they need wisdom, you can share an area of your own life. We all need lots of wisdom.*

6. *We often don't go to God for insight right away because we forget He's there. Or we doubt that He will really help us. Or we don't expect Him to speak in a way we can understand. Or we don't want to hear His answer. Generally, we're simply accustomed to doing things for ourselves in our own way.*

7. *Although Jesus says He wants us to come to Him as little children (see Matthew 19:14), He means we are to have the humility and openness of children, not remain permanently childish. His desire is for His followers to grow to maturity and learn to make wise decisions (see Hebrews 6:1–2). Those who are permanently simple-minded are gullible and easily drawn off the path God has for them. They don't bear as much fruit for Him in their lives.*

8. *Wisdom, like Jesus, isn't aggressive. She doesn't demand; she invites. She knows she has something valuable to offer—a feast of good guidance for anyone who responds humbly and gladly to her invitation. It's really worth the time to go to her house, sit down with her, and take in what she offers.*

9. *True love of the Lord is the high point and goal of wisdom. But the "simple" must start with the basics: recognizing that God deserves reverence and understanding, and they need to get out from the center of their lives and put God in that place. People grow to love the Lord as they experience His forgiveness, love, and guidance—but spiritual maturity begins with a healthy fear of and reverence for God.*

10. *The wise are grateful for rebuke and advice because they know it betters them, like iron sharpening iron. They want to accept rebuke or advice so they know how to correct their mistakes and avoid making new ones. Anybody who thinks he or she has reached the pinnacle of wisdom and doesn't err anymore is either simple or foolish. The truly wise are aware that they have a long way to go. Their fear of the Lord makes them humble and receptive to correction.*

11. *When we think of God as the Holy One, we think of His moral perfection. He is wholly good and can't abide the presence of wickedness even in small amounts. Thinking of this aspect of His character and our own persistent tendency to sin makes us fear His justice. We know we fall short. Fortunately, God is also extravagantly loving and has sacrificed His Son to deal with our sin, so we don't need to live in terror of His judgment. But we should always retain some of that healthy fear so that we don't take His love for granted.*

12. *Answers will vary.*

13. *Answers will vary.*

14. *Responses will vary.*

Session 4: Following God by Praying for Guidance

1. *Ask any group members who feel comfortable doing so to elaborate on any of the conditions they chose from the list.*

2. *Answers will vary. The goal is to bring to the surface the areas of life where the group members most need wisdom and guidance from God.*

3. *There are many actions people can take when the problems of life grow heavy. Some of us may attempt to escape the difficulties. Or we may frantically search for answers, become depressed, or get angry that we are in such a dire situation. But another option—if we have developed the habit—is going to God with our questions and then expressing our thanks to Him in spite of what we are facing.*

4. *The troubles and battles that we are enduring are part of a larger battle—a spiritual battle—and the way we respond to them can serve to glorify God. When others see followers of Christ respond to their difficulties in a godly manner, it makes them curious about what is different in their lives. The* *responses of believers can either point others to Jesus or away from Him.*

5. *Taking a moment to pray first can help us acknowledge our need for God and our trust that He will help us. This trust enables us to go about our work in dependence on Him. Also, God can guide the minds of believers as they think things out and make decisions. Just knowing He is involved in what we're doing will give us confidence.*

6. *There are many reasons why God's people often fail to go to God in prayer: We feel rushed and under pressure to finish tasks quickly. We have trouble slowing down enough to pray. We may doubt that God will hear our prayers or do anything if we pray.*

7. *Believing in God isn't a psychological state that we need to whip ourselves into. It's a relationship with a Person. If we honestly lack confidence in God, we can take that to Him and humbly ask Him to strengthen our faith. Honesty with God is of great importance, and our faith in Him will grow as we talk to Him. James is chiefly criticizing "secret doubts" that we aren't confessing to God. Those type of doubts undermine us.*

8. *Answers will vary. Make sure the group members know they don't need to be embarrassed about their doubts. Doubts are normal. Even King David expressed doubts that God would come through for him, as we read in Psalm 13:1: "How long, LORD? Will you forget me forever? How long will you hide your face from me?" The point is to be straightforward about our questions and fears, for they become weaker when exposed to the light. Remember, as the leader, it's not your job to "fix" other people. (Be sure to also discourage group members from trying to talk anyone out of his or her doubts.) You can ask follow-up questions to draw participants to say more about their doubts and where they come from, but don't try to resolve their dilemma. God can do this on His own.*

9. *God's goal is for His sons and daughters to grow to maturity. The Bible is clear that He is more interested in our spiritual state than in solving our problems. So God waits for us to engage in our side of the relationship, asking* *for what we need and believing with confidence that He is able to provide it to us. When we receive wisdom, He wants us to know it's from Him.*

10. *In verses 5–8, James says we are to not just ask for wisdom, but to ask trusting that God will provide it. Now in these verses, 22–25, James says we are not to just read the Word, but read it with a determination to do what it says. The Bible is a storehouse of wisdom, and we need to apply it, not just know about it.*

11. *The gospel requires the people of God to show love to others in a variety of ways. For example, the Old Testament presents the Ten Commandments, six of which speak to our treatment of and attitude toward others. In the New Testament, Jesus urges us to love our neighbors as ourselves (see Matthew 22:39), to love our enemies (see Matthew 5:44), and to turn the other cheek (see Matthew 5:39). Paul likewise asks fellow believers to encourage one another and build one another up (see 1 Thessalonians 5:11).*

12. *Answers will vary.*

13. *Answers will vary.*

14. *Responses will vary.*

Session 5: Following God by Shunning Worldly Wisdom

1. *Urge the group to keep their responses relatively brief. Some may have infuriating tales of worldly wisdom that they were taught at school, at home, or that they read on the internet. This is a fine place to start, because it affects how they interact with true wisdom, but you don't want your entire meeting to be about this.*

2. *Generally, the problem with false wisdom is that it masks itself as godly wisdom—it sounds good, so we tend to want to believe it. Unfortunately, if we act on it, we will find ourselves in worse straits—all because we didn't* recognize the difference between the true and the false. This is why we need to soak ourselves daily in the Bible, so that we can learn God's true wisdom and not settle for counterfeit versions.

3. If we fear God doesn't have things under control, we can be drawn into a fight, freeze, or flight response: either striking out in anger at a situation or person, feeling paralyzed and helpless, or running away in a panic. None of these is a wise response for a person of faith.

4. Some group members may be in a peaceful time of life, where it is easy for them to express gratitude to God. Others may be in more turbulent times, where they have a lot of doubts and confusion about why God isn't seemingly interceding on their behalf. Once again, make your group a safe place for people to share their stories and struggles, and to even admit they don't have as much faith or gratitude toward God as they would like to have.

5. If believers in Christ want to become more aware of God's abiding presence, there's simply no substitute for spending time alone with Him daily. We all need this—especially when we're dealing with things beyond our control. We need committed time with God each day to orient ourselves to true wisdom, discern false wisdom, and tune in to the Holy Spirit's guiding voice through prayer and the Word of God. We can also check in with Him frequently throughout the day, asking, "Jesus, please guide me in this situation."

6. Answers will vary. Some group members may respond that they have been asking God to show the way forward, but it seems He is taking His time to reply. This is a hard place to be in—but it is common (again, remember King David's words in Psalm 13:1). Encourage those who haven't yet received clear guidance from God to keep "asking," "seeking," and "knocking," knowing that God promises to His children that "everyone who asks receives; the one who seeks finds; and to the one who knocks, the door will be opened" (Matthew 7:8). And if you have non-believers in your group, take this opportunity to speak Christ's offer of salvation (without singling out anyone) and then guide your group *through the Sinner's Prayer as part of your conclusion to the meeting.*

7. *Some signposts of earthly wisdom include "lack of humility," which we've mentioned as being too focused on ourselves, our needs, and our problems. "Bitter envy" could be defined as an angry, demanding desire to possess what others have, and "selfish ambition" as a desire to get ahead (via money or power) that doesn't mind steamrolling others along the way. Self, self, self is the hallmark of earthly wisdom!*

8. *It's critical because worldly wisdom can easily tempt us to accept it as truth. God's wisdom may seem less attractive to us in the moment, but His wisdom will never invite us into bitterness, envy, or selfishness—it's always going to point us in a direction that is peace-filled, pure, and loving toward others. As Christians, we need to be aware that, at times, God will guide us to step out of our comfort zones, which—as the term implies—will not always be comfortable or alluring to us.*

9. *Each of the qualities James mentions in this verse is important for us to possess because they point us to God's pure ways. For example, God will always guide us toward the path that is "peace-loving" and "considerate" of others' needs. Worldly wisdom tempts us toward a different path—a selfish or destructive one. The Lord's voice will never be the one urging us to boast in our own strength; His Spirit will compel us to be "submissive" and "full of mercy" when it comes to our relationships with others.*

10. *James is stressing that worldly wisdom pridefully causes us to believe we are more in charge of our lives than we actually are. We can make all the plans we like—there's nothing wrong with that in and of itself—but we can't leave God out of the equation. When God's children humble themselves and seek His direction, they can be sure that their plans will succeed in the ways God intends, because they know that they are acting in His will.*

11. *This is the humble attitude of those who truly understand that life is fragile, and they could die before tomorrow comes. They know the Lord's will is sovereign* *and good, and they want to live in alignment with it. The person who says these words with conviction and honesty is in a position to receive God's direction.*

12. *Answers will vary.*

13. *Answers will vary.*

14. *Responses will vary.*

Session 6: Following God by Loving His Word

1. *Answers will vary. This is a chance to motivate the group members to spend some daily time in God's Word. As the leader, you should come prepared to share how time in the Bible has helped you know more of God's direction for your life.*

2. *Once again, you might want to lead off by talking about the obstacles you face—especially with busyness or the challenge of what to do with passages you don't understand. You may be able to recommend some study resources that can help the members read with understanding. For example, it might be useful to compare two Bible versions to get another reading of the same passage. A good, one-volume commentary can also be helpful. And you can look up lots of place names, people's names, and cultural references on the internet.*

3. *We're back to the idea of wisdom, which can literally be defined as the ability to think things through and apply proven principles to make good choices. Believers need to value this ability and not get frustrated when God doesn't give us "specific" instructions instantly at every turn in our lives.*

4. *God's Word contains many direct instructions on what to do and not do. But beyond this, the Bible provides guidance by simply letting us know who God is and what His purposes are. We learn to recognize how God thinks about things, what He values and doesn't value, and how He deals with people like us in the Bible. The more we see how He responds in situations, the more able we are to* *understand how He would have us respond in various situations.*

5. *Answers will vary, but God's Word can help us make right judgments about all sorts of issues. Allow the group members to respond to this question with a brief story, but don't get sidetracked at the actual issues themselves.*

6. *Here again, allow the group members to respond, but don't go into too much detail or get off track. One clear example to which most of us can relate is the temptation to judge others based on the money they have or the effort they invest in their appearance. We might also tend to judge them by what they do for a living or maybe even their political affiliation.*

7. *When the psalmist writes that he loves God's law, he is most likely referring to more than the list of dos and don'ts we find in the Bible. Rather, he is speaking of the peace that God's children receive when they know they are walking in His will and following the steps He has laid out for them. As Isaiah wrote, "The effect of righteousness will be peace, and the result of righteousness, quietness and trust forever" (Isaiah 32:17 ESV). To willfully do things that are contrary to God's commands always leaves believers in an unsettled state as we wrestle with our conscience. But walking in God's ways brings peace and helps every child of His grow in spiritual maturity.*

8. *As the group leader, consider reading aloud a portion of Matthew 5:21–48 as an example of the kinds of instruction Jesus gives His followers regarding how to live. His words are challenging and cannot be obeyed without the strength the Holy Spirit provides, but they are eminently practical and speak to the Christian's daily life. For instance, if we're wondering whether we should marry a certain person, we can get beyond romantic attraction and honestly ask ourselves whether this is a person who would take Jesus' words as a standard for behavior (and even more and more as he or she matures)? Or is this a person who would find Jesus' words foreign and unthinkable?*

9. *There are many ways to meditate on God's statutes. For instance, we could* take a small portion of Jesus' words each day, or a small portion of Paul's teaching in Ephesians 5–6, and keep reviewing it until we have committed it to memory. We can post meaningful verses that speak to us in prominent places where we will see them frequently. We can use a Bible app so that when we're standing in line at the store, we can reread our passage of the day.

10. *God's instructions may not always be easy, but they are always the right course for His children to take. God's instructions always lead ultimately to a good life. Also, we know instinctively when we read them that we are learning about a better way to live than the often mindless and selfish ways we see in the world around us. It's important to deeply reflect on how good these words are so that we become willing to try to live them.*

11. *Answers will vary. The goal here is to motivate the group members to dig into the Word for guidance—so they see how the Bible provides them with instruction on how to live.*

12. *Answers will vary.*

13. *Answers will vary.*

14. *Responses will vary.*

Session 7: Following God by Listening to the Spirit of Truth

1. *Most people have only a vague idea of who the Holy Spirit is. In truth, He is fully God, just as the Father and Jesus are fully God. He is like wind in its power and invisibility and like fire in its all-consuming power (see Acts 2:1–4). Yet, at the same time He is a person, not an impersonal force. The Bible states that He can be grieved (see Ephesians 4:30), sinned against (see Isaiah 63:10), and lied to (see Acts 5:3). Followers of Christ are instructed to obey His voice (see Acts 10:19–21) and honor Him in all they do (see Psalm 51:11).*

2. *Christians often feel under assault for their beliefs. However, as followers of*

Christ, we need to remember that the pressure we feel to conform to the world's values often comes about because the Holy Spirit is convicting the world of sin (see John 16:8–9). Our job is not to aggressively attack the world but to simply testify about what we know of God—and to do so with love but also firmness.

3. *As Christians, affirming our confidence in God can be as simple as saying a quick prayer throughout the day: "Jesus, I place my trust in You right now. Please guide me." We can also release anxious thoughts to Him and choose to act in loving and unselfish ways toward others. We can choose to not give in to fearful inclinations but instead step out in faith.*

4. *If you, as the group leader, have a good story to tell about the Holy Spirit coming through for you, be sure to share it to encourage the group. One thing that often keeps us from crying out to the Spirit is being unaware of who He is. In many churches, He gets less mention than Jesus and God the Father. Another thing that can hinder us is a habit of self-reliance.*

5. *Thinking of our tasks as things we "have" to do easily leads to negative emotions such as discouragement and frustration and resentment. However, thinking of our tasks in terms of things we "get" to do tends to spark positive emotions and open doors for creativity. For example, if we view volunteering at church as a "have to," it will feel like a burden. If we view it as a privilege to be serving in a capacity where we can help others, our entire attitude will be changed. It may come as news to group members that they can actually choose to adopt a frame of mind that doesn't at first come naturally, thanks to the Holy Spirit's work in the lives of believers!*

6. *The Holy Spirit is not a subordinate who answers to our every whim—He is God. Yet He makes Himself available to Christians and brings divine power to assist us in accomplishing things we could never do in our own strength. Just think of Jesus' command to "love your neighbor as yourself" (Mark 12:31). We could never do that without the Holy Spirit's divine empowering.*

7. *The Holy Spirit guides Christ's followers by reminding them of what God said to His people and what Jesus said to His disciples. We have God's teaching in the Bible as well—words that the Holy Spirit carefully communicated to each biblical writer. Now we need the Holy Spirit to bring to mind what we read—but we still need to read it! We can't expect the Holy Spirit to remind us of things we have never exposed ourselves to. By taking in the words of the Scriptures, we give the Spirit opportunity to bring those words back to us when we need them.*

8. *As previously stated, the word "advocate" in this passage means someone who defends and offers counsel to God's people. Help the group members think of situations in their lives where they are challenged to graciously speak up for Jesus and need wise words.*

9. *In John 14:6, Jesus says that He Himself is the truth. The Holy Spirit, being God as Jesus is God, can also be called the Spirit of truth. Truth is the essence of what they both offer—truth about how the world works, about the nature of God, about what a human life is for, and about the best ways to live. The context of this passage indicates that the Holy Spirit will continue the work of Jesus on the earth—leading unbelievers to the truth of salvation and leading believers to pattern themselves after the example and mind of Christ.*

10. *One way the Holy Spirit guides God's children is by giving them wisdom and understanding as they read the Bible and apply it to their lives. The Holy Spirit can illuminate a passage and help us comprehend what steps God is instructing us to take. In 2 Timothy 3:16, Paul writes that "all Scripture is God-breathed and is useful for teaching, rebuking, correcting and training in righteousness." The Holy Spirit even inspired the writers of Scripture as they penned the words of God!*

11. *If we accept God the Father and Jesus the Son as the authority in our lives, then we should accept the Holy Spirit as well, because He carries their divine authority. The three (known as the "Trinity") do not speak with* different voices—they are united and one in what they tell us. God wants us to know the Holy Spirit is as trustworthy as Christ and as trustworthy as Himself.

12. *Answers will vary.*

13. *Answers will vary.*

14. *Responses will vary.*

Session 8: Following God by Obeying the Holy Spirit's Promptings

1. *Answers will vary. It is likely that many of us internalized our parents' instructions by the time we were teenagers, and could thus could obey them without being "micro-managed." Most parents prefer it when their adolescent children learn what is expected of them—they like not having to issue as many reminders as they would to a young child! Still, there are times when a parent asks something unexpected of a teen.*

2. *Some Christians will recognize these promptings more easily than others. Usually, this prompting comes in the form of putting a principle in Scripture into practice in a particular situation. We can know it's His voice when it's consistent with the Scriptures and the wisdom of God.*

3. *Answers will vary. Listening to God involves making time to listen as well as learning to recognize His voice. We can't expect His Spirit to shout while we go about our daily business being preoccupied with other things.*

4. *Again, these promptings often come as a believer is searching the Bible for wisdom. They also come when the Holy Spirit brings to mind a passage that we read previously. Feeding our minds with Scripture gives us a storehouse of truth that the Holy Spirit can use to guide our thoughts and actions. Taking time to listen to Him in solitude is also important.*

5. *Answers will vary. The goal here is for group members to become more aware of any avenues of guidance they may have been neglecting.*

6. *Some people don't feel as if God responds to them when they pray. For believers in Christ, this can happen during certain seasons in our lives, and it's not necessarily our fault. When we are following God but are not consciously aware of being led step by step, it's an opportunity for us to trust Him and grow in wisdom. This can be scary and frustrating, but if we are searching the Scriptures, spending time in God's presence, and taking counsel from wise believers in Christ, we can have peace in knowing we've made ourselves as available as possible to God's guidance. One thing believers in Christ can be sure of is that eventually God will make His will known to us. But we must keep seeking Him as we wait.*

7. *Paul and his companions responded to these setbacks by simply taking steps to go where the Holy Spirit was allowing them to travel. We don't know exactly how the Holy Spirit blocked the team's way, but any number of obstacles could have led them to conclude the Holy Spirit had another plan for them. The important point is that Paul and his companions were able to discern these obstacles as coming from the Lord, and they realized that He was using the obstacles to point them on the path that they should travel.*

8. *This is one of the many passages that have led Bible scholars to conclude that God is a Trinity of three Persons in one undivided God. The Holy Spirit is distinct from Jesus, and yet He so closely speaks for Jesus that He can be called the Spirit of Jesus.*

9. *We can't know for certain, but visions are more common in Acts than they seem to be in the modern West. The Holy Spirit had blocked Paul before, so it is possible that he needed a clearer prompting than usual to take the step of crossing the Aegean Sea to get to Macedonia. Up to this point, he had stayed in the provinces of Asia Minor (modern-day Turkey).*

10. *Answers will vary. Participants may not have thought of those times as the Holy Spirit deliberately blocking their way. These are confusing situations for Christians, but they are good opportunities to draw closer to God and learn the spiritual benefits of waiting with expectancy.*

11. *Answers will vary. Allow the group members a few minutes to share any stories they have of how the Holy Spirit has done this in their lives as believers.*

12. *Answers will vary.*

13. *Answers will vary.*

14. *Responses will vary.*

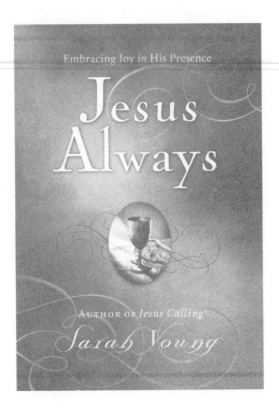

Also available in the
JESUS ALWAYS® BIBLE STUDY SERIES

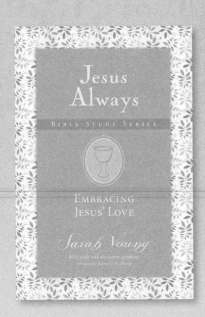

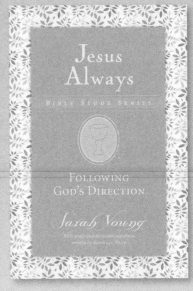

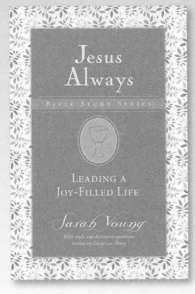

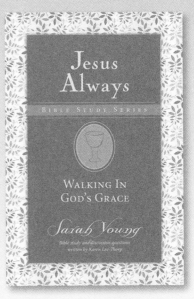

Also Available in the
Jesus Calling® Bible Study Series

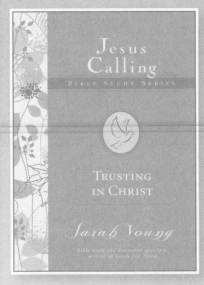

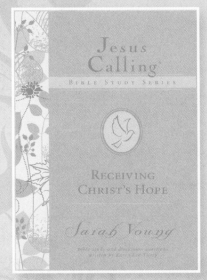

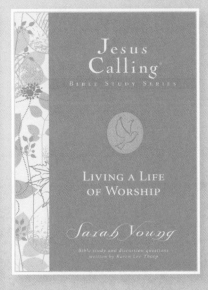

Also Available in the
Jesus Calling® Bible Study Series

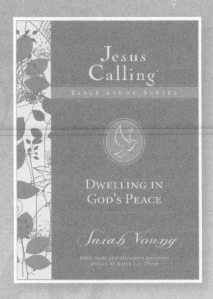

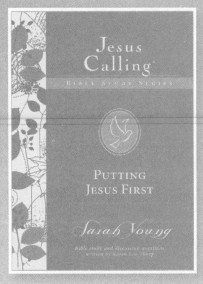

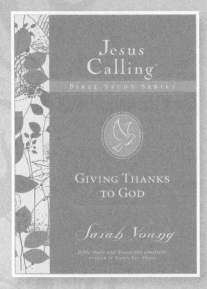

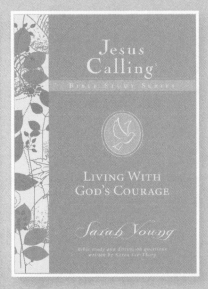

If you liked reading this book, you may enjoy
these other titles by *Sarah Young*

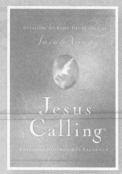

Jesus Calling®
Hardcover

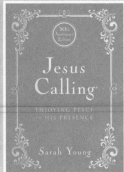

**Jesus Calling® 10th
Anniversary Edition**
Bonded Leather

Peace in His Presence:
Favorite Quotations from Jesus Calling®
Padded Hardcover

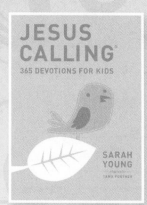

Jesus Calling® for Kids
Hardcover

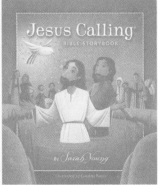

Jesus Calling® Bible Storybook
Hardcover

Jesus Calling® for Little Ones
Board Book